THE AGE OF
DECLINING TURBULENCE

Are Alan Greenspan's Projections Wrong?

Douglas N. Thompson

Research Associates

Christy Holt
Scott Goates

Other Contributors

Katie Clayton
Garry K. Ottosen
Phil Thompson

Published by Crossroads Research Institute, a nonprofit
operating foundation conducting research
on economic issues.

Crossroads Research Institute
807 E. South Temple, Suite 202
Salt Lake City, Utah 84102

Trustees:
Douglas N. Thompson
Garry K. Ottosen

ISBN: 0-9624038-4-9

I

Contents

Chapters

Chapter 1

ALAN GREENSPAN'S WORRIES

In his 2007 book, *The Age of Turbulence*, Alan Greenspan, former chairman of the Federal Reserve Board, expresses grave concerns about the near-term future of the United States.[1] When someone of his experience, stature, and capability expresses concerns about likely future problems, we must pay attention. This chapter examines Greenspan's worries and argues that the two major problems he foresees will be largely avoided. And then, on an even more positive note, the rest of the book describes powerful forces that are driving the United States and the world to a much improved future with *declining* turbulence.

Greenspan's First Worry: Inflation

If Greenspan's worry about inflation, which he expresses forcibly, is realized, we are headed for extended turbulence similar to that which accompanied and followed the accelerating inflation of 1965-1980. The stock market will be depressed, long-term Treasury bonds will have double-digit yields, and the economy will be sluggish. Inflation may not seem important when viewed against the background of the present recession, but it will become relevant when the economy achieves a vigorous recovery. The inflation threat will be real.

Greenspan has an abiding fear that inflation will accelerate because the Federal Reserve *will be prevented by Congress or the president from raising short-term interest rates to control inflation*. At one point in his book he almost forecasts that that will happen. He writes, "The 4.5 percent inflation rate, on average, for the half century following the abandonment of the gold standard is not necessarily the norm for the future. Nonetheless, it is probably not a bad first approximation of what we will face" (p. 482). An *average* inflation rate of 4.5 percent, double the Federal Reserve's apparent target, means that we will have some periods of inflation higher than 4.5 percent with consequences similar to those of the 1970s

1

and early 1980s. Greenspan suspects that 10-year Treasury notes could yield 10 percent, in contrast to their present (early 2009) yield of less than 3 percent.

If government succeeds in preventing the Federal Reserve from raising short-term interest rates to curb inflation, the inflation rate will surge far above that 4.5 percent average. And the interest rate on the 10-year note will rise above that expected 10 percent. This book claims that neither the Congress nor the president will succeed in preventing the Federal Reserve from stabilizing the inflation rate in the United States most of the time near the 2-to-2.5 percent range. Look at the contrast between the current inflation and monetary environment and that which prevailed in the mid-to-late 1960s when the Johnson administration put great pressure on the Federal Reserve to hold down interest rates even though inflation was accelerating.

First, a sizable percentage of economists at that time were arguing that we could *permanently* reduce the unemployment rate by allowing faster inflation. Accelerating inflation was initially greeted with equanimity rather than panic. Few economists hold that view today.

A second major difference in the inflation environment between the 1970s and the present can be found in monetary theory. If you doubt that we have learned much about inflation control, read the monetary history of the late 1960s and 1970s. Monetary theory was a mass of confusion. What should be the relative importance of monetary and fiscal policy? How often should the Federal Reserve intervene? What indicators should guide Federal Reserve action? And especially, how important is the money supply in the inflation process? Some wild proposals were advanced and received considerable support. We do not now have a complete understanding of inflation control, but it is far superior to the confusion of the 1970s.

Third, the United States had had little experience with *peacetime* inflation. Inflation had mostly been a product of *major* wars and had ended shortly after the wars had ended. People generally did not realize that the economy had changed and that seriously accelerating inflation could exist in peacetime or during minor wars. The price of bonds declined significantly as inflation accelerated in the late

1960s and as the market rate of interest rose. But stocks continued rising for about five years until the approach of the 1970 recession. That recession was precipitated by Federal Reserve restraint. It was the first meager attempt to control inflation.

During that five-year period there was no great sense of panic and little understanding of how difficult it would be to bring inflation under control. But now we have the harsh experience of the 1970s to remind us what inflation can do if not attacked early. Any significant effort by Congress or the president to stop the Federal Reserve from restraining inflation would be greeted by panic in the bond, stock, and foreign exchange markets. Memories of the 1970s inflation problems are still vivid. Neither Congress nor the president would want to be seen causing such a panic by limiting anti-inflation action. Overt effort by government to prevent the Federal Reserve from raising interest rates to restrain inflation would cause a much greater decline in bond and stock prices than would be caused by the actual raising of interest rates because it would destroy *predictability*. Many policy makers in government have apparently learned that lesson.

Inflationary forces are certainly not dead, but the ability of government to seriously limit the Federal Reserve's power to contain inflation is at least comatose and probably dead. In this matter, Greenspan's worries are probably largely unwarranted, and that makes a huge difference in making decisions involving the economic outlook and in valuing stocks.

Still another facet of inflation control should be considered—our ability to learn. Throughout this book I argue that Americans, and much of the world, have gone through many learning experiences in which capitalism has moved from a defective childhood to a rambunctious adolescence on the way toward a much-improved maturity. Learning to control inflation is one of these learning episodes. Greenspan apparently does not share that view. He writes, "It is possible that Congress has observed the remarkable prosperity that emerged in the United States and elsewhere as a consequence of low inflation and has learned from this happy circumstance. But I fear that containing inflation through higher interest rates will be as unpopular in the future as it was when Paul Volcker did it more than twenty-five years ago" (p.479).

3

The Coming Inflation Test

The improved monetary policy of the last quarter century has not been adequately tested. A major test lies ahead. Not long after the recession that followed the subprime mortgage debacle ends, we will face a serious inflation threat. At least four factors will be involved.

First, the federal deficit. In 2009 the federal government is running a deficit above a trillion dollars. Will this deficit cause inflation to accelerate? Not likely in the face of the intense competition that exists in an economy operating well below full capacity. However, if large deficits persist as the economy recovers, they will produce excessive demand and accelerating inflation as the intensity of below-capacity competition fades. But when the economy recovers, the deficit will automatically shrink. Tax *revenues* will rise along with increasing incomes. The need for government investment in the banking system and the automobile industry will decline and probably reverse. Government stimulative spending will no longer be needed. Tax *rates* will rise as many of the Bush tax cuts expire.

Nevertheless, continued budget deficits and inflation dangers may come from demands for increased spending. Huge expenditures will be required to finance the coming effort to achieve universal health-insurance coverage. That effort could increase federal spending by more than $100 billion a year when fully implemented. Additional demands for education, infrastructure, and other needs will keep the pressure high for more government spending. If government should allow high deficits to continue after the economy recovers, it would deserve to reap the excessive inflation, Federal Reserve restraint, rising interest rates, decline in stock prices, and perhaps even a double-dip recession that would follow. That unpleasantness might come just as the election of 2012 approaches. I believe that government has learned better than to invite those consequences.

Will the huge volume of new money *already created* by the recent extreme federal deficit, and by aggressive Federal Reserve policies to alleviate the banking crisis and recession, cause inflation to accelerate in a year or two? Part of this new money has been invested in banks and automobile companies and will be repaid. Much of it will be held by businesses and consumers to build up their depleted store of assets resulting from bad-debt losses and shrinkage in the value of homes. Only part of it, probably small, will get into the pool of liquid assets that could create demand-induced inflation after business recovers.

A second inflation threat may come from a *weakening of competition built into the structure of the economy*, that wonderful disciplining force that helps control inflation. A weakening of structural competition might come through protectionism that impairs foreign competition, a strengthening of labor union ability to organize and press demands for higher wages, or increased government regulation that boosts compliance costs.

The United States' enthusiasm for free international trade has recently declined, as evidenced by congressional failures to ratify bilateral trade agreements. Frequent protectionist comments have been made this past year by prominent Democrats who now have increased power in Washington. Even the *perception* of a return to protectionism is damaging to business planning for projects that would increase international competition and help control inflation.

Structural competition might also be limited by changes in labor union policies. Labor union influence in the Democratic Party is palpable. Unions are now calling for government to guarantee greater ability to organize and to strengthen their bargaining power. *Significant* increases in union power would accelerate wage increases. Those increased wages would not be taken from corporate profits but would be passed on to the consumer through increased prices, enhancing the inflation threat.

Increased government regulation that boosts business compliance costs is another possible threat to the inflation-inhibiting power of structural competition. The president and his supporters have called for a large array of new programs that, *if badly designed*, could increase compliance costs and accelerate inflation. Among them are: providing health insurance for the currently uninsured, making Medicare and Social Security solvent over the long term, reducing greenhouse-gas emissions, rehabilitating our long-neglected infrastructure, and vastly improving education.

The third inflation threat will almost certainly be important. Before the onset of the current recession, the world's economies were growing so fast that they were pushing up against the availability of the earth's known resources to support even the existing rate of output, let alone continued growth. Chart 1.1 shows how the world's growth rate has shifted upward from an annual average of about 3.5 percent to an average of about 4.5-to-5 percent. The increase was not a result of accelerating growth in advanced economies but of an acceleration in growth of emerging and developing economies. They have been growing recently at about 7-to-8 percent per year. The International Monetary Fund estimates that that growth rate will continue, although interrupted occasionally by recessions.

The increased growth rate has been a result of the shift toward capitalism by emerging countries. This development has years to run and will remain a major inflation threat for many years. We have used up the excess production capacity of the world's known resources that we have usually kept in reserve. Time will be required to discover new resources and to develop substitutes. After we recover from the current recession, the rate of growth of the world's economies may have to be moderated by central bank restraint to avoid inflation. Not much imagination is required to recognize the increasing need for resources as the 85 percent of the world's population now living in developing countries achieve

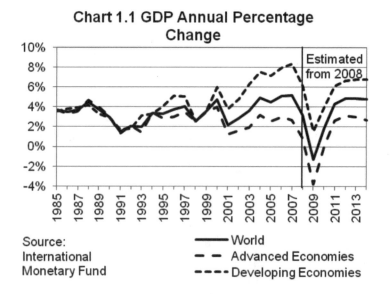

Chart 1.1 GDP Annual Percentage Change

Source:
International
Monetary Fund

—— World
— — Advanced Economies
---- Developing Economies

advanced-country lifestyles.

A fourth inflation threat may come from Asia. Greenspan argues that we have been living in a relatively low-inflation environment for several years thanks to a flood of low-priced goods produced by Asia's cheap labor. As labor costs in Asia rise, our import prices will also rise, reducing their past disinflationary impact. This is partly true, but that past increased competition from Asia has created a long lasting rise in the intensity of structural competition in the United States. It produced a sharp decline in labor union membership and in union bargaining power. Corporations could not meet high union wage demands because they could not increase prices in the face of Asian competition. Union popularity and power declined.

Greenspan also argues that the extremely high personal savings rate in Asia will decline. That decline will be dramatic if the "joys" of American-style consumer credit become available. An increased world-wide demand for goods and a decline in investment funds available for business will follow. But the decline in Asian personal saving will likely be at least partially offset by a major increase in the personal savings rate in the United States. As described in Chapter 5, that increase in the personal savings rate could increase total saving by several hundred billion dollars each year now that the housing bubble has burst. A decline in the Asian savings rate may not be inflationary.

These four inflationary forces will provide a stringent test for the new Federal Reserve policy. The Fed will not pass the test perfectly, but its performance should be far superior to that of the late 1960s and 1970s. That performance must be carefully watched in coming years to pick up any sign of a weakening of anti-inflation resolve.

The preceding analysis should have made it clear that the causes of inflation extend far beyond the long-repeated mantra that "inflation is always and everywhere a monetary phenomenon." That is a demand-side explanation. As Chapter 4 describes, inflation is caused by "too much demand relative to the ability of the existing intensity of competition to restrain price increases." That includes both demand-side and supply-side causes of inflation.

Two Scenarios

In Greenspan's scenario, government will likely prevent the

Federal Reserve from raising interest rates enough to slow inflation as inflationary forces develop. The following chain of events is *implied* in that judgment. Expectations of further acceleration of inflation will increase. With loss of confidence in Federal Reserve restraint, inflation will get out of control until a crisis forces the Federal Reserve to act, bringing deep recession with high unemployment. The turbulence of this inflationary period and aftermath will look a lot like the turbulence of 1965-1985.

In my scenario, as inflation accelerates, the Federal Reserve will tighten money enough to curb that inflation. Since inflation will be attacked early, only moderate, temporary tightening will be required. No one should underestimate the importance of attacking inflation early *before inflation habits become entrenched*. Those inflation habits are difficult to dislodge. The serious double-dip recession of 1980-83 was required to break the entrenched 1970s inflation habits. Escalating wage norms are of special importance since wages and benefits make up nearly two-thirds of production costs. In the late 1960s and the 1970s, workers came to expect larger *percentage* increases in wages each year, and business managers came to expect that they would be forced to grant those escalating percentage increases. They planned their pricing policies accordingly. "This is our best contract yet," was the typical announcement made by unions after each major contract settlement.

Since that inflationary period, workers' expectations have, on average, been much lower. They have generally expected wage and benefit increases around 3-to-4 percent each year. With productivity (output per hour worked) increasing about 2 percent a year, inflation should be kept within the apparent Federal Reserve target of 2-to-2.5 percent. But even though inflation remains within Federal Reserve targets, we will always face the danger of inflation creep.

Inflation Creep

Although government will not likely prevent the Federal Reserve from raising interest rates to slow inflation, the Federal Reserve may, on its own, adopt policies that will allow the inflation rate to creep upward. In the three or four years up to mid-2008 we experienced an episode of inflation creep. The Federal Reserve targeted *core* inflation—headline inflation minus food and energy. Core inflation was controlled, but headline inflation was well above target.

Prices of food and energy over the years have fluctuated widely. Sharp price rises have usually been offset by subsequent declines. Therefore, the core inflation rate has quite properly been considered to be a more reliable guide for day-to-day Federal Reserve policies. But things have changed. If food and energy prices do not decline as much as they have in the past, offsetting that multi-year excessive growth in headline inflation, the Federal Reserve may have to pay more attention to the headline inflation rate.

Greenspan's Second Worry: Growing Income Inequality

Greenspan has another worry, even more serious than the inflation problem—growing income inequality. He sees growing inequality as being driven by the demand for "ever-greater skills as one new technology builds on another," coupled with the breakdown of our elementary and secondary school system. And he sees the possibility of disaster unless we fix our schools. He writes: "The impact that fixing our school system would have on our future levels of economic activity may not be easy to measure, but unless we do so and begin to reverse a quarter century of increases in income inequality, the cultural ties that bind our society could become undone. Disaffection, breakdowns of authority, even large-scale violence could ensue, jeopardizing the civility on which growing economies depend" (p. 468). Now that's a *serious* worry. Greenspan has little to say about how to fix the school system, but he briefly mentions the voucher system as a possible improvement.

I suggest that income inequality will *not* be significantly reduced. Dealing with the problem of income inequality will require much more than fixing the schools since the *causes* of income inequality are much more profound than the breakdown in our school system. Differences in inherited genetic capabilities and early nurturing account for a great deal of the income inequality in our complex technological society. Income inequality is an inevitable part of capitalism. People with widely divergent genetic and nurturing heritages sell their unequal skills in the competitive market. Unequal incomes are certain to follow.

Even though income inequality will not be *greatly* reduced, the grievous social difficulties feared by Greenspan will not likely ensue. Those difficulties have so far been largely avoided and will continue to be so, by our modifying the *results* of income inequality. Those results of inequality include the suffering that follows poverty and inadequate health care, inadequate access to education, distress stemming from accidents and the afflictions of old age, and many others. In short, the social services that make up the social safety net are efforts to ameliorate the *results* of income inequality. Putting it more bluntly, social services have saved capitalism by preventing the unraveling of our social fabric that Greenspan fears. The social safety net is an essential part of capitalism.

Immigration

Immigration provides Greenspan with a second possibility (after school improvement) for reducing income inequality. He suggests that we open our borders to unlimited immigration of professionals and other skilled workers. The high wages and salaries available in the United States would attract so many skilled workers that present high wages and salaries of skilled workers would stop rising, partially shrinking income inequality. Chapter 8 argues for a step in this direction by a major expansion of the H-1B visa program to provide for the immigration of a small number of people with special skills. Could this program be expanded enough to reduce income inequality substantially? It seems doubtful. We must rely on improving the operation of the social safety net to ameliorate the consequences of income inequality.

The Social Safety Net

Greenspan, in the last two pages of his book, quite properly worries about *excessive* use of social safety nets. It is a worry that surfaces in bits and pieces throughout the book. He blames this excessive use of social safety nets mainly on income inequality: "As awesomely productive as market capitalism has proved to be, its Achilles' heel is a growing perception that its rewards, increasingly skewed to the skilled, are not distributed justly" (p. 505).

He cites Europe as an example of excessive use of safety nets: "Social safety nets exist virtually everywhere, to a greater or lesser extent. By their nature, they inhibit the full exercise of laissez-faire, mainly through labor laws and income redistribution programs. But it has become evident that in a globally competitive world, there are limits to the size and nature of social safety nets that markets can tolerate without severe negative economic consequences. Continental Europe, for example, is currently struggling to find an acceptable way to scale back retirement benefits and worker protections against job loss" (p. 504).

Indeed, such examples in Europe are abundant. The Netherlands has often been cited for its high disability rolls. Sweden also suffers from this problem. Swedes are extremely healthy. But according to *The Wall Street Journal*, 13 percent of the working-age population receive a disability benefit—the highest proportion in the world.[2] This is often attributed to a system that is too lax and does little to verify claims.

France provides an interesting example of "protected" labor markets. (Some other European countries are similar.) France suffers from high unemployment, especially among young workers. The youth unemployment rate is over 20 percent. Strict labor laws are in place to prevent employees from being fired. This was intended to *help* the unemployment situation; but actually it makes hiring workers much more risky, and keeps unemployment high.

The United States has also had examples of the overuse of the social safety net. Chapter 8 describes how a major relaxation of rules governing availability of welfare in the late 1960s resulted in a huge increase in its use and cost. In the 1990s, eligibility requirements were tightened, resulting in a major movement from welfare to employment. This episode is often cited as a successful application of tough love.

It seems to me that the history of social safety nets provides a lesson. Income inequality in market economies will not be quickly or dramatically reduced. Greenspan thinks it will increase. The public generally perceives that inequality to be unjust. Since income inequality cannot be greatly reduced and will continue to be perceived as unjust, public pressure will continue to be strong, and perhaps will increase, for social safety nets to ameliorate the *results* of that inequality. Social services will continue to be provided, some of them unworkable. Those who see a great future for a mature capitalism must recognize the problem of income inequality and use their best efforts to find *workable* policies to ameliorate the *results* of inequality. The design of those policies must not be left entirely to those who do not appreciate market capitalism—nor understand how it works. Although the social safety net is often badly designed and sometimes used excessively, it saves us from the breakdown of the social fabric and other possible dire consequences Greenspan has described. Our rational self-interest demands that we improve the safety net. It has a valuable function.

For capitalism to survive in a democracy, a capitalist-friendly government must be elected and reelected. A capitalist-friendly government is not likely to survive unless that government provides sufficient social services to ameliorate the results of the inevitable, capitalist income inequality.

The Medicare Part of the Safety Net

Greenspan, along with most economists, worries about the inability of government to finance Medicare in the face of the coming surge of people entering the age of high medical needs. He points out that financing Medicare's present program by increased taxes is probably not feasible since the amount of required funds will be so great. He expects the Medicare funding imbalance to be met by reducing benefits to the more affluent. Future Medicare *benefits*, in his view, will be concentrated in the middle- and low-income groups. He may be right, but some other approaches will likely be required. They are described in Chapter 8.

Greenspan Didn't Worry About a Banking Crisis

Writing in 2006-07, Greenspan expressed no worry about a possible breakdown of the banking system. He expressed some unease about the risks involved in subprime and Alt-A mortgages, but was willing to accept those risks to expand home ownership. He felt that any attempt to expand regulation of the financial system would be futile. Like almost everyone in government and the financial community, he failed to "connect the dots." He didn't see the connection between the speculation-driven home-price bubble, the huge quantities of defective mortgages that could avoid default only if home prices continued to surge, the securitization of those mortgages that placed them in excessive quantities in banks and insurance companies around the world, and the worthless system of insuring those mortgage-backed bonds by a new device called credit default swaps. It is astonishing that almost everyone in our financial institutions and government, even with access to extensive information about the developing danger in the financial system, failed to connect the dots.

Greenspan's Other Worries

Greenspan, of course, has other worries, several of which are shared by most economists. Among them are the danger of a return toward protectionism, *overuse* of progressive income taxes to reduce income inequality, and wild-card events such as a lethal flu pandemic or a nuclear terrorist attack on American soil. None of these possible developments should be dismissed lightly.

Summary

In summary, Greenspan is enormously pessimistic about inflation and the problems involved with the growing inequality in income. He sees periods of rapid inflation and, although he doesn't spell it out, his inflation projection implies a deep recession required to break such an inflation. He is essentially saying that we will likely return at least partly to those nasty inflationary days with a recessionary aftermath that tormented us between 1965 and the mid-1980s. His worries about the possible consequences of growing income inequality are tempered only by the slight possibility that a dramatic solution to our education problems will be found and that we will open our doors to a vast flood of skilled immigrants.

To me, Greenspan's somewhat dismal near-term outlook stems from a conviction that governments will be unwilling to learn. Furthermore, he shows a lack of confidence in the efficacy of competition, particularly competition among governments to attract capital investment with the desirable actions that that competition will engender. The extraordinary successes that I believe will flow from that competition are described in Chapters 2 and 3.

Although Greenspan perceives a rocky road in our near future, he closes with a note of optimism. "It is not an accident that human beings persevere and advance in the face of adversity. Adaptation is in our nature, a fact that leads me to be deeply optimistic about our future. Seers from the oracle of Delphi to today's Wall Street futurists have sought to ride this long-term positive trend that human nature directs. The Enlightenment's legacy of individual rights and economic freedom has unleashed billions of people to pursue the imperatives of their nature—to work toward better lives for themselves and their families. Progress is not automatic, however; it will demand future adaptations as yet unimaginable. But the frontier of hope that we all innately pursue will never close" (p. 505).

This first chapter has taken a negative approach. It has attempted to demonstrate that Greenspan's two main worries will not likely be realized (government will not prevent the Federal Reserve from raising interest rates to curb inflation, and growing income inequality will not lead to a breakdown in the social fabric). The rest of the book takes a positive approach. I attempt to show that powerful forces are driving the world to a much-improved capitalist century with declining turbulence.

******

Readers especially interested in investment should now turn to Chapter 10. It is a moderately technical discussion of stock investment in the capitalist century. After reading that chapter, return to Chapter 2 and read the rest of the book including a reread of Chapter 10. Reading that chapter twice, once before and once after reading the rest of the book, will be helpful, *but only to an avid investor.*

Chapter 2

THE AWAKENING

Optimism is not in fashion these days. But skeptics fail to recognize that in the last 20 years of the twentieth century an economic awakening occurred. That awakening ushered in a capitalist century and set the world on course for what will surely be by far the grandest period of economic and political development this world has ever seen, even though it will be marred by new problems and a few setbacks. The first part of the awakening was a wake-up call delivered by the lure of capitalist abundance.

The Lure of Capitalist Abundance

The lure of capitalist abundance is a powerful force for change. In the last 20 years of the twentieth century, capitalist abundance was so attractive, compared to the shabbiness of government-managed economies, that governments of countries containing over half the population of the world began, or accelerated, a shift toward capitalism. China and Russia were the most dramatic, but there were several others. That display of the power of capitalist abundance created several other mighty forces that are transforming the world. This book will tell the story of how these forces, set in motion by the attractiveness of capitalist abundance, will likely play out in the capitalist twenty-first century.

Competition among governments to attract the capital investment that is necessary for a modern capitalist economy is a second dominant force for change. It was dramatically intensified by the proliferation of would-be capitalist countries. Capital investment is in limited supply. Governments must compete with one another to provide the most favorable environment to attract that investment. That competition among governments is a powerful force. After beginning slowly, it is intensifying and is remaking the world.

One can hardly imagine more favorable circumstances for the design of twenty-first-century institutions than those provided by intense competition among governments to attract capital investment. Governments must provide a rule of law to protect private property and the primacy of contract. They must maintain peace and tolerance to allow investors and others to move freely and safely around the country. The education of workers is, of course, mandatory. Responsible fiscal policy and essential bank regulation are required. Corruption must be minimized by reducing government regulations that provide an army of regulators with the power to extract bribes in return for favorable decisions. Borders must be opened to trade and investment to increase competition and productivity. All these improvements need not be complete to *begin* attracting capital, but a trend must be evident, and a willingness to continue that trend must also be evident. The capitalist revolution has barely begun. Not one of these new would-be capitalist countries has come close to completing the necessary improvements to the investment environment. That will be an ongoing project for the twenty-first century. Capitalist abundance will be on display in a growing number of countries. The lure of that abundance will keep most governments on course.

Improving Capitalist Stability

In the second part of the awakening, governments of many existing advanced capitalist countries, together with a number of developing countries struggling to become capitalist, made substantial progress toward *solving the problem of economic instability*, a defect that had long plagued capitalist countries. Prior to World War II, that instability had been manifest mainly as financial panics and long periods of unemployment, the Great Depression of the 1930s being the worst. After World War II, instability surfaced mainly as inflation that could be brought under control only at the cost of serious recession and unemployment, as required in 1980–83 in the United States to end the 1970s' inflation. Since the early 1980s, governments have made great progress in learning to control inflation without producing deep recession. Improved economic stability has made capitalist abundance even more attractive.

Our ongoing progress in correcting capitalism's instability should finally lay to rest the belief held by so many for so long that periods of high unemployment, deep recession, and crippling inflation are an inevitable part of capitalism. We are now (early 2009) experiencing another serious recession. This recession was caused by our failure to maintain a high quality of credit in our financial system, not from the necessity to curb inflation. As Chapter 5 describes, this credit failure and its recessionary aftermath will provide another learning experience to improve the future stability of our capitalist system.

Benefits of the Awakening

We have already begun to see important declines in turbulence thanks to the spread of capitalism and the greater stability of capitalism. The general decline in warfare and conflict has been startling. A study by a team of scholars at the University of Maryland's Center for International Development and Conflict Management (cited by Fareed Zakaria in his book *The Post-American World*) came to the following conclusion: "The general magnitude of global warfare has decreased by over sixty percent (since the mid-1980s), falling by the end of 2004 to its lowest level since the late 1950s."[3] Much of this decline in warfare among and within states is undoubtedly due to the end of the Cold War. The end of the Cold War was part of the shift toward capitalism resulting from the lure of capitalist abundance.

The improvement in capitalist stability was dramatically evident in the United States as inflation dropped from a high of nearly 15 percent in 1979 to a 1990s average of about 3 percent. Other advanced capitalist economies showed similar inflation performance. Chapter 4 explains how capitalist countries managed to bring inflation under much greater control without producing deep recessions.

But we have just begun to reap the benefits of the awakening. Most of today's problems can be traced to one or more of four sources, past or present: authoritarian governments, socialist economies, institutionalized religious intolerance, and defects in capitalist economies. All four of these sources of trouble are being driven out by competition among governments to attract capital investment and by the correction of defects in capitalist economies, particularly in the control of inflation and unemployment. By the end of the capitalist twenty-first century, international warfare as we have known it will largely be gone. Most areas of extreme poverty that now exist in Africa and elsewhere will have disappeared. Strongly authoritarian governments will no longer exist, except perhaps in a few small countries. Intolerance as now promoted by religious institutions will be but a memory. Of course, intolerance by many individuals will remain. Periods of economic stagnation will be infrequent and mild. Total world population will have risen from the present near 7 billion to slightly over 8 billion by midcentury. It will then have leveled off and begun a long-lasting decline to significantly below its present level.

This book spells out in some detail how the forces unleashed in the awakening make the realization of this outlook highly probable even though it must now seem improbable to most. Much of it will likely be realized long before the end of the capitalist century. But the timing is not certain. If we fail to recognize and seize the many opportunities newly opened by the capitalist revolution, we will remain too long as victims of a stagnating pessimism.

In summary, two related forces will be most important in transforming the future. The lure of capitalist abundance will continue to turn governments toward genuine capitalism. And the proliferation of capitalist countries will create a dynamic competition among governments to attract capital investment. That competition will mold the institutions of the twenty-first century.

In the hundred years that began with the period of awakening, those two forces will extend a highly productive economic system with spectacularly improved technologies to 85 percent of the world's population. That 85 percent of the population has languished in relative poverty under government-managed economies with old-fashioned technologies. They have lived under autocratic governments. With the new economy they will gradually earn better civil liberties and greater political rights along with their vastly improved wealth. No empire, civilization, or superpower of the past can come close to serving as an analogy to help predict how the events of the unfolding capitalist twenty-first century will play out. They will be unprecedented.

I will add only the following qualification to the above

projections. We exist on this planet at the sufferance of mother nature (a.k.a. this savage, unpredictable earth)—the final authority. She is certainly the ultimate host of the capitalist century. And she may, in an unmotherly way, disrupt the outlook with lethal flu pandemics, climate change, or even a civilization-ending mega-volcano or asteroid collision. Perhaps we are becoming a special annoyance to mother nature and are inviting retribution by aiding and abetting climate change.

Freedom Will Follow Capitalism

The extension of political rights and civil liberties will be one of the most important benefits to arise from competition among governments to attract capital investment. Each year, Freedom House, a nongovernmental organization, carefully analyzes every country in the world and classifies them into various categories of freedom based on the political rights and civil liberties of their citizens. Clearly, political rights and civil liberties have improved in the last few decades. Today 46 percent of the world's population live in "free" countries, compared with 39 percent just ten years ago. Most capitalist countries are free, grading well in civil liberties and political rights. Most government-managed economies are not free. They have extended few political rights and few civil liberties to their citizens. We can expect the ongoing shift toward capitalism to add impetus to the move to democracy and civil liberties, as it has over the past few decades. Chapter 3 describes the ways in which the shrinkage of the size and activities of government that follows a shift to capitalism makes democracy and increased individual freedom almost inevitable. Authoritarian governments will fade away.

The Coming End of International Warfare

The ending of international warfare is the most audacious, and yet splendid, projection that can reasonably be made from an analysis of the forces described in this book. But it is justified. The worldwide extension of an *improved* capitalism is creating a mighty *interdependence* among countries that will make international warfare obsolete. Already the average country relies on imports for about 25 percent of its supplies and also on exports to provide jobs for a large percentage of its workers. Cross-border investment is growing dramatically. Many companies and individuals have more assets invested in other countries than they do in their own. That interdependence is not a recipe for warfare. It is a recipe for peace.

But there is another important facet of this interdependence. The capitalist expansion is creating a *community of common interest*. All major countries and many minor countries are capitalist or trying to become capitalist. They all have a common interest in the working of the international capitalist trading system. *Each government is learning that its economy will not perform well unless the entire system works well.* Contrast that situation with the twentieth century. Major countries and many minor countries were divided into two camps, militarized and with opposing goals. That was the essence of the Cold War.

The potential for peace implicit in today's capitalist community of common interest should not be underestimated. Anatol Lieven and John Hulsman in their 2006 book on international relations, *Ethical Realism*, argue that this common interest of the major powers has, with proper nurturing, the *potential* for creating what they call the "Great Capitalist Peace."[4]

By the end of the capitalist century, and probably much sooner, warfare between all but the smallest, laggard countries will be as unthinkable as is a war now between France and Germany who fought the last of several wars just over a half century ago.

An important note: Growing international interdependence and the growing capitalist community of common interest certainly *do not* give the United States cause, at this time, to disarm or feel safe from terrorist attack. What they do mean is that common interests are growing, and the United States must use every effort to ferret out those common interests in every corner of the world and nurture them as best we can with firmness, patience, and understanding. We must proceed in all our international relations with the conviction that world peace may soon be possible.

Recognizing the existence of the burgeoning international interdependence and the capitalist community of common interest is important, but an understanding of the powerful forces that are driving their development is even more important. A description of those forces must await Chapter 3.

Governments Can Learn

One more item should be emphasized regarding that 20-year period of awakening from 1980 to 2000. *We have learned that governments can learn.* Democratic governments are easy targets for criticism. We forget that they are attempting to perform what seems like an impossible task, to bring together in a workable coalition hundreds of interest groups with different and often conflicting objectives. When they don't perform as well as we would like, we throw up our hands and complain, "They'll never learn." But governments learned some things well in that 20-year period of awakening. Before the awakening, developing countries operated with some variant of socialism. Advanced countries operated with some variant of a *defective* capitalism. The awakening moved both camps toward an evolving and improving capitalism. Competition to attract capital investment, driven by the desire to gain capitalist abundance, should keep them learning.

Government is an essential part of capitalism. It performs functions that only government can perform, such as maintaining adequate, but not excessive, aggregate demand and sufficiently intense structural competition. But only the market can make those billions of day-to-day decisions necessary to organize production and distribution. Capitalism is not just an economic system. It is a political-economic system, a partnership between the market and the government, each doing that which only it can do.

In the capitalist century ahead there will be bumps and potholes but no repeat in most advanced countries of the Great Depression of the 1930s or the inflation of the late 1960s and 1970s.

Understanding Adolescent Capitalism

Many Americans believe that capitalism is mature, approaching old age. That is wrong. Capitalism is not old or mature. It is young, an adolescent. It only recently slipped out of a long defective childhood into adolescence in that 20-year period of awakening. That adolescence is mystifying many observers, as adolescents have mystified observers for generations. But surely the greatness of a mature, adult capitalism still lies ahead.

The long period of childhood that preceded adolescent capitalism was marred by two major defects. Its footprint on the world was small, mainly North America and Europe. *Effective capitalism demands wide, international trading areas* and the interdependence that wide trading areas create. And it had not learned to prevent the instability of depression and inflation. In the current period of rambunctious adolescence, capitalism is correcting both of those defects.

Capitalism faces a formidable challenge—to bring a large measure of peace and prosperity to nearly 200 countries with disparate cultures, scores of religions, hundreds of languages, and thousands of unavenged atrocities harboring simmering hatreds. But the forces driving capitalism are strong, particularly the growing competition among governments to achieve capitalist abundance by attracting capital investment. Most countries are still in their capitalist childhood. Some have entered adolescence, but only a few have mature capitalism in sight.

Few people recognize that the past accomplishments of capitalism, as important as they were, were the accomplishments of a *juvenile* and an *adolescent* capitalism. Even fewer people are aware of the benefits in the form of peace and prosperity that a worldwide, mature capitalism will deliver in the coming century.

In the international arena, capitalism has met a number of opposing ideologies. It has survived, partly because it was able to improve itself. Its antagonists have included socialism, communism, mercantilism, fascism, periods of excessive government regulation, and a host of opposing religious beliefs. There is no reason to think it will not survive its current most obvious challenger—extremist Islam.

The worldwide triumph of capitalism by the end of the century is highly probable. It will be driven by the lure of capitalist abundance and the competition among governments to attract capital investment. But it will not come without setbacks, and many problems remain to be solved.

A young reader might assume from this chapter that life in the coming years will be easy—no danger of being drafted into the army, no Great Depression, no long periods of inflation followed by deep recessions, rising real incomes. Unfortunately, life will not be easy. The world will change at an even more rapid rate. Life will still be a struggle. Competition will be intense. Pressures to perform will be great. Some companies and whole industries will disappear. New jobs will usually be easy to find for those with skills, but sometimes not in the same industry or the same area. Having a marketable skill or skills will be the best security in this dynamic, competitive environment. Unfortunately, as I will point out in Chapter 8, the inadequacy of genetic and nurturing heritage will keep out of reach for many the growing opportunities becoming available for those who are more abundantly endowed. An unknown, but probably small, fraction of the populace will be unable or unwilling to adapt to a dynamic, competitive capitalism, even one that of necessity will become more humane. They will become wards of the nanny state, in prison or on welfare.

Problems Yet to Be Solved

The following chapters will look at solutions to some of our remaining problems.

Chapter 3 provides an expanded view of the impact of those creative, commanding forces that are transforming the world. They are even more intriguing than this chapter has indicated.

Chapters 4 and 5 offer a detailed description of how we have improved capitalism's stability, and how we can improve it even more.

Chapter 6 examines the hopes and fears related to China's growing importance in the world. It also describes an interesting collision that is building as capitalism meets the Muslim Middle East.

Chapter 7 explores the fear that America will not be able to compete with cheap-labor countries using our modern technology. It puts that danger in perspective.

Chapter 8 faces up to the puzzles raised by providing social services. Health care, education, and other social services are a growing problem in capitalist countries. Social services now absorb such a large part of a capitalist country's total output that improved solutions to the problems are mandatory. Governments are competing with one another to find those solutions. Success will be important in determining the success of an entire economy. This chapter argues that developing countries need a large measure of *capitalist* compassion.

Chapter 9 describes how the controlling forces involved in the capitalist expansion will have an overwhelming impact in slowing population growth.

Chapter 10 describes how the financial markets will likely behave in the capitalist century.

Chapter 11 portrays the impacts of the most important controlling force—the *accumulation of human knowledge*.

Chapter 3

FORCES THAT WILL MOLD
THE TWENTY-FIRST CENTURY

In the capitalist twenty-first century, the many governments of countries responding to the lure of capitalist abundance will lose a massive amount of power. The coming period could properly be called the age of declining governmental power. Governments will experience a loss of power in at least three ways.

First, *loss of power as employer.* In government-managed economies, a large part of the population works for the government. Government bosses have the right to hire, fire, discipline, and spy on employees. Workers develop an understandable fear of the power of government. In a market-managed economy most people work for private employers. Workers lose much of their fear of government.

Second, *loss of power to the marketplace.* Governments in nonmarket economies have had great power to determine what goods and services will be produced, where they will be produced, how they will be produced, and how they will be distributed. In a market economy that vast decision-making power is wielded, directly or indirectly, largely by consumers. Furthermore, in a market economy, financial markets give stockholders and bondholders the power to register quick and dramatic objections to government policies, especially policies perceived to be inflationary. Security holders register their complaints by selling their stocks and bonds. Declining security prices raise fear of recession and lower government popularity.

Third, *loss of power to voters as democracy follows capitalism.* Governments must please the majority of voters. They must keep the economy operating reasonably near to full employment. That means they must avoid inflationary policies that bring central bank restraint, slow growth, and increased unemployment. Of course, many other failing policies can lead to voter dismissal of a government.

We should put this loss of governmental power into historical perspective. Throughout most of recorded history the power to control human affairs has been largely in the hands of a few powerful individuals at the head of governments, thus spawning the "Great Man" theory of history. That has been changing and will continue to change. The control of human affairs is coming more under the authority of *vast impersonal forces* to which governments must constantly defer. These forces operate through the marketplace and the voting booth. The core methodology of this book is to identify these controlling forces and to appraise their strength. Forecasting allows nothing less.

Forces Dominating Change

Chapter 2 described two related dominant forces, the lure of capitalist abundance and the competition among governments to attract capital investment. The sequence of development is clear.

• The lure of capitalist abundance brought a major geographic extension of would-be capitalists in that 20-year period of awakening.

• The proliferation of would-be capitalist countries increased the competition among governments to attract capital investment.

• That more intense competition is creating favorable investment environments, which have most of the characteristics necessary for a peaceful and prosperous world. The improvement of investment environments will continue throughout the twenty-first century. The stark differentials between capitalist abundance and the shabbiness of government-managed economies will keep most would-be capitalist governments on course. Authoritarian governments, not the people, have usually made the decision to turn toward capitalism. Those governments have seen in capitalism the road to wealth, power, and prestige for themselves and for the people they govern. All governments will eventually learn.

Additional controlling forces that limit governments will be described in this chapter and throughout the book. They operate through capitalist markets and through democratic elections. Some are products of technological change. The ongoing accretion in the power of these forces to manage human affairs, replacing the power of autocratic governments, will be one of the great epochal transformations in human history as it nears completion by the end of the capitalist century. The enormity of this ongoing transformation is not properly recognized. Those both in and out of governments who underestimate the power of these forces are making grave mistakes and are likely to forego exciting and valuable opportunities.

What Must Governments Do to
Attract Capital Investment?

To repeat, *one can hardly imagine more favorable circumstances for the design of twenty-first-century institutions than the intense competition among governments to attract capital investment.* Most of the things governments must do to win out in the never-ending struggle to modernize are well known. They were introduced in Chapter 2 and include at least five categories.

1. Governments must provide a workable, generally accepted rule of law (including an independent judiciary) to protect private property and the primacy of contract. The term "rule of law" has been such a commonplace listing as a requirement for a decent society that one can easily pass it by without realizing what a glorious thing it can become when properly implemented. *It provides predictability.* When protecting private property and the primacy of contracts, it becomes the foundation of capitalism. It makes possible the appraisal of risks and rewards by entrepreneurs and workers alike, thus providing incentives for action. The rule of law is in contrast to the uncertainty of rules laid down by an authoritarian figure that are often changed by a changing authoritarian whim. The rule of law is essential to attract capital investment from abroad and is also necessary to attract capital investment from within a country to create the thousands of small businesses required for a workable economic system. Equally important, the rule of law regarding property and contracts can set a precedent and become a rule of law protecting civil rights. It can evolve.

2. An environment of peace and tolerance is necessary to allow buyers and sellers, investors and entrepreneurs, teachers and students to move safely and comfortably around the country, and indeed around the world. No one wants to invest in a country

that is likely soon to be involved in war, civil or foreign. Tourism especially requires tolerance, and tourism has become a major source of funds that developing countries can use to acquire capital equipment. Not surprisingly, intolerant Iran has languished near the bottom of the list of countries that are ranked by foreign tourist income as a percentage of GDP.

3. Governments must maintain considerable fiscal responsibility, avoiding unnecessary spending, taxation, and borrowing. Appropriate bank regulation is an important part of this fiscal responsibility. Failure in the fiscal arena shows up as inflation, excessive budget deficits, widening current account deficits, bank failures, and eventually unemployment and stagnation. Bond, stock, and currency markets nowadays levy severe penalties on governments for lax fiscal policies, discouraging capital investment in the process.

4. Besides providing an appropriate legal and fiscal framework, a government must provide a decent human environment in order to attract the best capital investment. Of course, citizens must be properly educated and trained. This is especially true when a country graduates from its initial comparative advantage of providing cheap labor and moves into the competition for designing, selling, and maintaining sophisticated products.

5. Corruption must be minimized. Transparency International, a nongovernmental organization, conducts periodic surveys to estimate the perception of corruption in various countries. Clearly, the most corrupt countries attract the least foreign investment. Corruption is most prevalent when government regulation is extensive, providing an army of regulators with the power to extract bribes in return for favorable decisions. Ration coupons, housing permits, travel authorizations, business licenses, job opportunities—these are examples of the authorizations that government employees can trade for bribes in countries where governments maintain extensive control of an economy. Minimizing corruption generally requires the shrinking of government regulation of economic activity.

Industrialized countries, as well as developing countries, are faced with this competition to attract capital investment. The competitive pressure to improve the investment climate never ends.

Governments of industrialized countries are under pressure to continue making all those improvements that developing countries must make to attract capital investment. When they fail to do so, they see their own firms channel investments to friendlier environments, and they attract little offsetting investment from abroad.

Of course, no country has to make all the above-listed reforms before it can begin to attract capital investment. But some progress must be made and a trend toward an investment-friendly environment must be evident. Sooner or later, an investment-friendly government will arise in all countries as the pressure to achieve capitalist abundance becomes irresistible. Countries simply cannot go far toward achieving capitalist abundance without becoming part of the international investment community. Unfortunately, in a number of countries, such a government will arise later rather than sooner. Nevertheless, movement toward reform is unmistakable.

Some governments have adopted those policies with alacrity, knowing that they would lead to prosperity. Other governments are being dragged, reluctantly, into the capitalist century, as competition drives them to action. The policies necessary to attract capital investment will lay the foundation for both capitalism and democracy, thus determining the basic environment for the twenty-first century. By adopting capitalist principles, developing countries will catch up with today's advanced countries, which will continue to improve their capitalist systems. What an enormous increase in production, prosperity, and well-being that will produce! The 20 years of awakening did, indeed, touch off a revolution.

The importance of this new competition among governments to attract capital investment takes on a special glow when contrasted with the earlier, mostly military, competition among governments that has plagued the world for so long.

The Changing Nature of
Competition Among Governments

Few will deny that a vicious competition among governments has prevailed during most of recorded history. Much of the rivalry was driven by the *desire to achieve wealth, power, and prestige* for the governments themselves and for the countries they ruled. Often, the desired power was to extend religious domination. The acquisition of land and its natural resources, together with the people who worked the land, was the primary method of adding to wealth, power, and prestige. But the supply of land is relatively fixed. To add to territorial holdings meant seizing land from some other government. And that usually meant war, the main expression of intergovernmental competition throughout recorded history.

Rivalry among governments still prevails and is still being driven largely by the *desire to achieve wealth, power, and prestige.* The big difference is that the technique for achieving those goals has changed dramatically. Whereas the control of land and the people working the land was once the measure of success, nowadays the quantity and quality of *productive capital* is becoming the critical measure. Adding to land meant taking it from another government, usually resulting in war. Adding to productive capital more often results in cooperation of governments through international trade and through the functioning of the international investment community, even though considerable bickering arises at the many points where competitors meet. *Surely the ability of governments to satisfy the drive for wealth, power, and prestige without resorting to war is one of the most valuable gifts of modern technology and capitalism.* As more governments become aware of the necessity to make their countries attractive places for capital investment to achieve those long-standing goals of wealth, power, and prestige, the world will be a more peaceful place in which to live.

The Geographic Law of Specialization

A powerful force that I call the geographic law of specialization has driven, and will continue to drive, the world toward larger trading areas. Therefore, it is a critical factor in driving the world toward greater interdependence and more durable peace. The critical need for wider trading areas is being driven by technological change, and is therefore very reliable. The law simply states: *The greater the variety of goods produced, the wider the trading area necessary to obtain efficient specialization.* In agricultural-handicraft economies, a trading area of just a few miles was adequate to find specialists for most of the limited items used. Today, the extensive variety of products requires a worldwide trading area to find specialists that can efficiently produce each of the many required products.

Developing technology is increasing the variety of desired and needed products. No country or group of countries will be able to find the specialists for efficient production without *extensive* trade beyond existing borders. A market needs more than one specialist for each product. It needs enough producers to provide a competitive discipline. The wide variety of products makes that impossible for any single country today. The expanding variety of products will pressure the world toward greater economic integration. The continuation of this force, driving wider trading areas (and interdependency), is assured because it is based on continued technological change, a reliable development.

Looking at the record of the last few years, one might conclude that a large proportion of the governments of the world have discovered the geographic law of specialization. They are now struggling to bring their countries into larger and better free trade areas by bilateral and regional free trade agreements (FTAs). They are discovering that economically no country can remain alone. Large free trade areas make production more efficient, and increased competition helps keep inflation in check. To repeat, this movement is building a greatly increased interdependence. It will also strengthen that capitalist community of common interest where each government knows that its country performs well only when the system performs well. Prospects for international peace are improving dramatically.

The Business Roundtable has documented the recent growth of bilateral and regional FTAs. Eight years ago there were an estimated 130 FTAs. Today there are approximately 300 FTAs around the world with many more in active negotiation. Today, more than 50 percent of world trade occurs through FTAs. The widening of free trade areas has just begun. The geographic law of specialization is driving governments to much wider free trade areas. Almost every major country in the world is actively negotiating new FTAs, and some are enormously ambitious. Although FTAs have generally begun by countries expanding trade to next-door neighbors, like NAFTA in North America and Mercosur in South

America, governments are now becoming much more ambitious in their plans and preliminary negotiations. China, for example, is considering an FTA that would cover nearly all of Asia. An FTA for all of the Americas has been proposed.

These trading areas will likely meld with one another. Companies and individuals in each country are investing in countries far beyond existing trading areas. And the sovereign wealth funds of several governments are also investing in far distant countries. The need for wider trading areas is driving us toward an economic one world.

The United States is lagging behind most other major countries in establishing FTAs. It will fall behind its competitors if it does not begin to negotiate more free trade agreements. When an American company sells to a country that has formed a free trade agreement with another country but not with America, the American company typically faces higher tariffs than its competitors, as well as more limited access to services markets. Also, by allowing other countries to take the lead in negotiating free trade agreements, America will find itself having to eventually conform to business precedents and standards set by others. Other countries are also negotiating more *investment* treaties than the United States—agreements focused specifically on the investing environment available to international trading partners.

Worldwide trade agreements would be far better than bilateral and regional trade agreements, but the need for wider trading areas will not wait. These new FTAs are filling that need. Key partners and competitors of the United States—the European Union, Japan, China, India, Brazil—are all in extensive negotiations to increase their efficiencies and competitiveness by enlarging their trading areas. The United States must also enlarge its free trading area.

The record clearly demonstrates the relentless need for wider trading areas produced by the geographic law of specialization. In the past two decades world trade has grown nearly twice as fast as world output and shows no sign of slowing. Governments will soon recognize that all nations must eventually be integrated into the world trading community. We are being driven toward interdependency. Time is on the side of peace.

World Order from the Bottom Up

The twenty-first century will surely become a capitalist century. What kind of world governance will accompany world capitalism? Many idealists have dreamed of establishing a world government that would create, interpret, and enforce international law, and rule the population of the world. That is a top-down approach. It will not happen in the capitalist century, if ever. National governments will not yield their sovereignty to a world government easily. However, small moves toward improving world order are emerging from the bottom up. That is appropriate because it is the way that capitalism has largely evolved.

Each bottom-up move toward world order begins with a specific *problem*, such as the need to reduce barriers to international trade, facilitate international financial transactions, reduce confusion among accounting standards, or combat crime. Each of these problems is met by *spontaneous action*. That action may be initiated by a small group of governments. Or it might start with groups of people from several countries trying to find solutions to the same problems. These groups might be regulatory agencies, central bankers, law enforcement officials, professionals such as accountants, or others both in and out of governments. A couple of important examples will demonstrate how international governance from the bottom up can evolve.

The World Trade Organization (WTO) provides an ideal example of how such a spontaneous action may arise. Following World War II, the nations of the world undertook major initiatives to establish global organizations that would work to prevent future conflicts through top down orders. It was in this postwar climate of top down governance that the United Nations, the International Monetary Fund, and the World Bank were born. Attempts were made to establish an International Trade Organization, but when the U.S. Senate failed to ratify the ITO treaty, negotiators were left with only a patchwork of partial treaties known as the General Agreement on Tariffs and Trade (GATT). GATT was a treaty, not an organization. The purpose of GATT was to benefit the signatories in their trading arrangements. There was no explicit attempt to create, interpret, or enforce international law, just a collection of countries agreeing to a mutually beneficial set of rules and a rudimentary dispute settlement system. The agreement provided only that the contracting parties would jointly deal with disputes between individual contracting parties.

Of course, as the GATT developed, the dispute settlement system evolved as the contracting parties progressively codified and sometimes also modified the procedural dispute settlement practices. A system developed whereby expert panels would hear disputes and write independent reports with recommendations and rulings for resolving the dispute. Upon approval by the GATT council, these reports became legally binding, and a large and important body of jurisprudence was created. That body of jurisprudence grew much like the common law grew in England.

At the conclusion of the Uruguay round of trade negotiations, in 1995, GATT was transformed from a treaty to a formal institution, the World Trade Organization (WTO). Along with this transformation, perceived weaknesses in the dispute settlement system were strengthened. This dispute settlement system has been actively used in the years following its development.

The WTO has become the de facto body governing world trade without any sort of a top-down development. Various nations came together with the desire to improve their individual welfare by increased trade. They took it upon themselves to include enforcement provisions in the trade agreements. Because enforcement provisions often require interpretation, trading nations developed a system for adjudicating disputes. This system has been codified until it now carries with it the force of international trade law. Nations respect the WTO ruling, even when such rulings are not in their favor. They do this not only to avoid penalties but also because recognizing the legitimacy of the WTO allows them to bring complaints when they feel that they have been wronged. Thus a system to help bring order to international trade was born from the bottom up by spontaneous action of a few governments.

The Basel Accords are another example. They were established by a committee of central bankers from the G10 countries who were trying to develop standards and guidelines dealing with credit risk in order to bring stability to the international fiscal markets. Although the Basel committee has only 27 member countries, its standards are widely respected throughout the world, and globally more than 100 countries have adopted (at least nominally) the Basel prescription.

Anne-Marie Slaughter of Harvard Law School, writing in *Foreign Affairs*, suggests that existing governments are "disaggregating into separate functionally distinct parts. These parts—courts, regulatory agencies, executives, and even legislators—are networking with their counterparts abroad, creating a dense web of relations that constitute a new transgovernmental order. Today's international problems—terrorism, organized crime, environmental degradation, money transfers, bank failures, and securities fraud—created and sustain these relations." Ms. Slaughter sees an important role for these transnational networks in improving the world order.[5]

The World's Problem-Solving Capabilities

No one can know what problems the world will face in the capitalist twenty-first century. But the world's problem-solving capabilities are improving. What determines problem-solving capability? *The existence of a large number of capable participants with an opportunity to innovate, and under competitive pressure to do so, provides the best environment for problem solving.* As competitive market economies spread around the world, these conditions will expand in the private production sector, guaranteeing a widening flow of new, better, and less expensive products and services to solve long-standing problems such as human disease. But the more exciting prospect is the new competition among *governments*.

No forecast of the economic and political outlook for the United States and the world more optimistic than the ones made in this book is likely to be found anywhere. What do I see that pessimistic forecasters do not? I have greater confidence in the ability of governments to learn. To repeat, the best conditions for problem solving (learning) exist when many participants have the freedom to innovate and are under competitive pressure to do so. *All three of the conditions in that statement have improved dramatically in the recent years of the awakening.*

Freedom to Innovate

For most of the period since World War II, the problem-solving ability of many governments was under the constraints

35

of *socialist dogma and the Cold War*. Socialist dogma allowed little experimentation. But those constraints were shattered with the fall of the Berlin Wall leading to the collapse of the Soviet Union. The disclosure of the abysmal performance of the Soviet economy—that paragon of socialism—dealt a near-fatal blow to the already wilting socialist dogma that had shackled policy making in many countries for decades. The end of the Cold War also freed many governments whose policies had been chained to the requirements of the particular Cold War camp to which they were tied. A new sense of freedom to try innovative approaches appeared. A new sense of dynamism arose. The world is now changing at a faster pace, bringing new problems related to the transition to new policies. Governments have far greater opportunity (and pressure) to innovate than they had under socialist dogma and the Cold War. I wonder how many people fully appreciate the significance to government of this recent outbreak of freedom, innovation, and change produced by the awakening.

Large Number of Participants

When the Great Depression struck, there were just a handful of reasonably well-established capitalist countries. Furthermore, most of the economists in those countries had learned their economics out of the same textbooks. Consequently, few innovative approaches to solving the problem were devised until the Depression had done great damage. But now there are many reasonably well-established capitalist countries with a variety of cultural backgrounds, each one trying to find a superior solution to current problems.

The chances of solving the problems generated by evolving capitalism are improving as the number of capitalist governments increases, each trying to outperform the others. For example, look at the variety of approaches for dealing with fluctuating foreign exchange rates. They have varied from free-floating rates to fixed rates. Recent experience appears to indicate that relatively free-floating rates are better, except in very special circumstances. Fixed exchange rates have frequently been disastrous and have largely been abandoned. This type of experimentation among competing governments will be the wave of the future. It should vastly improve the problem-solving capability of governments as capitalism proliferates.

Far more governments are now involved in designing market-managed economies than ever before. The majority of governments have accepted the need to achieve capitalist abundance and have recognized (often tentatively) the need to make some change toward a market-managed economy. Each government faces its own particular set of circumstances and problems, so each government has to design a slightly (or vastly) different approach to development. Innovation is essential. Yet, with so many countries involved, each government has examples—some good, some bad—in each stage of development to look to for suggestions. There are now many varieties of competitive-market economies. There will be more. They arise as many participants experiment with new approaches to solving problems.

Competitive Pressure to Perform

Governments face serious rivalries in their race to gain wealth, power, and prestige. As described earlier, intergovernmental rivalry nowadays plays out more in the economic and social spheres than in the military sphere as it once did when wealth, power, and prestige were usually gained by taking territory from some other government. But that rivalry among governments is still very real and will force governments to take painful steps to solve their problems.

We have moved a long way toward the environment of having many reasonably capable government participants with opportunities to innovate and under competitive pressure to do so. Every act of governance now must face critical comparison to its counterparts designed by competing governments in many other jurisdictions. The most successful ones are eventually copied.

The Capitalist Alternative

Just the existence of the capitalist alternative is making compromises between antagonistic governments more attractive than they were during that long-stagnating period dominated by socialist dogma and the Cold War. Sometimes conflicts between governments have remained unresolved for years. The North Ireland conflict lasted a century. Sometimes conflicts are resolved by war. In the future, conflicts will, happily, more often be resolved by compromise.

When two antagonists face each other over some problem, such as the conflict between India and Pakistan over Kashmir, a peaceful compromise can be achieved only when *both* sides recognize that the status quo is *intolerable* and that *total* victory or *near*-total victory for one side is highly unlikely. As long as the situation is considered tolerable and one side thinks that one day it will be able to achieve victory, no compromise is possible. The status quo continues to fester. But when the status quo becomes intolerable and the prospect of all-out war is even less tolerable, compromises can be achieved.

The Kashmir conflict, for example, is becoming intolerable because both sides are becoming aware of the benefits they can achieve if the conflict is resolved. If peace is established, India and Pakistan can more successfully prevail in the competition to attract capital investment and become prosperous capitalists. The existence of this far better alternative makes the status quo intolerable and compromise possible. All around the world, simmering conflicts that have been tolerated because no alternative seemed to be available, now are beginning to appear intolerable because they are hampering the ability to attract capital investment and achieve capitalist abundance. Compromises should proliferate in the capitalist century.

The Changing Distribution of Income

How will the spread of capitalism affect the distribution of the world's rapidly growing wealth and income, both among countries and among individuals? The output and income of some developing countries like China and India have been growing much faster percentagewise than have the output and income of advanced countries. These countries have used their cheap labor, together with modern technology, to reap substantial competitive advantages in the world markets. But their wages are rising rapidly, and that cheap-labor advantage will diminish. Soon these rapidly growing countries (along with present-day advanced countries) will have to turn to present-day laggard, poverty-stricken, slowly modernizing countries for the low-cost labor necessary to produce high-labor-content goods. Then those laggard countries will join the group that is gaining on the advanced countries. The income gap between rich and poor countries will be dramatically narrowed during the twenty-first century. This narrowing has already begun.

As for income distribution among individuals, right now there are billions of poorly paid, unskilled (or lightly skilled) workers in the world. They include less-talented people and many naturally-talented people who never had the opportunity to get the education and training required to command better-paying jobs, even if such jobs were available. But cheap-labor-competitive countries are being forced by competition to provide better education and training and will gradually attract capital investment that will provide better jobs. Therefore, as the twenty-first century develops, there will be far fewer unskilled workers in the world competing for the same jobs. Fast-forward five or ten decades. Who in the United States will do the drudge work on farms or in cities when there are few immigrants or guest workers to do that work? Who will do the menial work in factories when cheap goods can no longer be imported in huge quantities manufactured by cheap labor in developing countries? The less talented will be doing the drudge work both on farms and in cities, but with far fewer extremely low-paid unskilled workers around the world to compete with, the less-talented workers in the United States will command relatively better pay.

Impediments to Modernization

The pressures to turn to capitalism to achieve the freedoms, the attractive job opportunities, and the wealth of market-managed economies are powerful, but so also are the well-known impediments. Those impediments include many authoritarian governments, entrenched bureaucrats, monopolists in both labor and product markets, and others who are *initially* hurt by a turn to a competitive economy. Impediments of a social nature include ideas, habits, customs, religious convictions, and embedded hatreds that are difficult to dislodge. But many countries are overcoming these obstacles and are building the investment-friendly environments necessary to achieve capitalist abundance. They are setting performance standards by which other governments are judged. The necessity to attract capital will intrude upon most decisions each government makes. Decisions will often be painful. Governments will have to compromise cherished traditions and temporarily alienate some of their people. The pressure to do so will be great.

There is no *realistic* alternative to modernization by attracting capital investment. The alternatives so far chosen by some governments (or by the people they are trying to govern) would, if continued, keep their countries in poverty, intermittent military conflict, and hopelessness, while they watch a large and growing share of the world move rapidly onto the road toward modernization with its wealth, freedoms, and opportunities. Those alternatives to modernization by attracting capital investment are not realistic. They will eventually be abandoned just as socialism is being abandoned in China, Russia, and Eastern Europe.

If the forces driving modernization are so powerful, does the nature of existing governments really matter? Of course it does. The wisdom, or lack of wisdom, of present-day leaders will determine how long and how painful the transition to capitalism will be.

Several present-day nonmodernizing countries are caught in a Malthusian trap. Rapidly growing populations are pressing against relatively fixed production capabilities. Standards of living are stagnant or declining. The only way to break out of this trap is to adopt the policies necessary to enter the competition to attract capital investment to increase production. That will not be easy. Countries such as Iran, whose leadership is staunchly resisting significant change, are inviting an eventual, sudden change in leadership. If delayed for long, such change could be violent.

Although impediments to capitalism often seem unyielding, we are entitled to look beyond the prevalence of entrenched hatreds and misconceptions, beyond the prevalence of unscrupulous and self-serving governments, and focus on the many places in the world where competition among private producers and competition among governments are making great progress.

Relapse?

Prior to World War I the world basked in a sense of optimism. Trade was expanding. The world had been relatively peaceful for decades. Productivity was surging with rising standards of living. The future looked bright. Then came the war, ushering in hyperinflation, the Great Depression, Hitler, World War II, socialism, and the Cold War. If some currently unexpected problem comes along equivalent in seriousness to the twentieth century's Great Depression, will capitalism be able to solve it? Or will competitive capitalism suffer another long setback like the twentieth century swing to socialism, which was in large part a result of the perceived failure of capitalism in the Great Depression? Many historians quite properly consider the possibility of a similar relapse in the twenty-first century. But it's not likely.

The juvenile capitalism of that earlier time was primitive. The few countries that professed to be capitalist were ignorant of some of the basic requirements of successful capitalism. Most of them did not understand how to design workable money and banking systems, or how to prevent serious inflation or deep depression. Furthermore, that primitive capitalism had not had enough time to produce the rule of law, the civil liberties, and the democratic governments necessary to maintain peaceful, prosperous societies. Interdependence was far weaker than it is now. In the United States, for example, in 2008 imports plus exports accounted for about 31 percent of GDP. That contrasts with about 10 percent of GDP in 1914 when the twentieth century began to fall apart. The improvement of capitalism since the Great Depression, the ongoing extension of capitalism to many new countries, and the correlative extension of democracy and civil liberties make a repetition of that devastating twentieth century relapse unlikely. Capitalism has, during the twenty years of the awakening, entered an adolescent stage and will gradually move into a mature stage in the capitalist century ahead.

Forces Driving History

Projections in this book sound like they are meant to be inevitable. Of course that would be presumptuous. But the projections are meant to emphasize that the *long-term* future will be determined more by the working out of *vast impersonal forces* than by the behavior of any one individual or small group of individuals.

As indicated at the beginning of this chapter, history-making decisions over the millennia have often been the product of the hunger for power, greed, religious inclination, or whims of some autocratic figure. But mainly in the last century, and especially in the period of awakening, history-making decisions have become more the product of impersonal forces that no autocrat or ruling clique can long defy. These forces derive their power from the masses of people exercising their freedom of choice in the marketplace and at the voting booth. In summary, three dominant forces have been described in this chapter:

First, most people and governments want to gain capitalist abundance. The lure of that abundance is turning governments toward capitalism.

Second, competition among governments to attract the necessary capital investment will mold the institutions of the capitalist century.

Third, very wide trading areas are an absolute requirement to gain capitalist abundance. The widening of trading areas will lead to interdependence and peace.

Other forces are described throughout this book:

• Accelerating scientific discoveries and technological inventions thanks to the increasing number of scientists and engineers, and the growing importance of scientific and technological competition, will maintain high productivity growth throughout the century.

• Accelerating shift of population from farm to urban settings will bring a sharp decline in the fertility rate and the start of a long-lasting major decline in the world's population.

• Three forces described in Chapter 8 are driving rapid changes in the U.S. health care system.

• Chapter 10 describes forces that are driving interest rates and stock prices.

• Chapter 8 describes the major forces behind the increasing demand for social services.

On a very long-term basis, the accumulation of human

knowledge can be usefully considered as the *major* controlling force. Its impact on history will be described in the final chapter.

And what is ultimately behind these decision-directing forces? The people! They will dominate decisions through the ballot box and in the marketplace by their decisions as to where to work, where to live, what to buy, and for whom to vote. So the future of human society will depend on the *nature* of human beings, who, as a group, are coming a little closer to becoming masters of their fate. That nature is being exposed. Cynics, of course, will worry.

Chapter 4

SOLVING CAPITALISM'S
INSTABILITY PROBLEMS, PART 1

Before World War II the major instability problems in the United States were financial panics, depression, and unemployment. After World War II, instability surfaced mainly in three forms: inflation, the slow economic growth required to *contain* that inflation, and the deep recessions required to *break* excessive inflation as in 1980-83. In that 20-year period of awakening at the end of the twentieth century, we made giant strides in our ability to maintain relatively low inflation while maintaining relatively rapid growth. This chapter and Chapter 5 will argue that these developments will be long lasting and can still be improved.

Two Requirements for Noninflationary Growth

The spending of money for goods and services (demand in the marketplace) is the necessary *initiator* of business activity. It activates the placing of orders, the hiring of workers, and the paying out of income. It creates customers. Without adequate spending for goods and services by consumers, businesses, and governments, nothing much gets done. We have periods of slow growth and recession. But spending is not enough. We must also have intense competition. Competition is the *controller* that channels spending into the efficient production of goods and services rather than into price increases. *The intensity of competition sets the limit* as to how far spending (and the growth rate) can be expanded without being dissipated into wasteful and counterproductive inflation. More intense competition allows more spending and therefore creates more jobs and faster growth.

In short, *inflation is caused by too much demand in relation to the ability of the existing intensity of competition to restrain price increases.* That is a much more comprehensive and accurate statement than the mantra that has been repeated for years: Inflation is always and everywhere a monetary phenomenon.

To maintain rapid noninflationary growth, then, we must proceed on three fronts.

1. Sometimes demand is so strong that it exceeds the ability of existing competition to hold prices in check. We cannot allow inflation to accelerate as we did in the late 1960s resulting in the inflationary 1970s. So we tighten money. That action has a dual impact on inflation. It reduces total demand, and it increases below-capacity competition. A description of this process is the first topic of this chapter.

2. Sometimes competition built into the structure of the economy is inadequate to restrain inflation when the economy is operating at a full employment level. This condition requires improvement in the many factors that determine structural competition. Opportunities to do so are almost always available. Improving structural competition should be a continuing program. A description of those opportunities makes up the second part of this chapter.

3. Sometimes demand is inadequate to keep the economy growing as fast as it could grow without accelerating inflation. We call these periods recessions. We must be able to increase demand to bring quick recovery. Chapter 5 will point out that this can be done quite easily with monetary stimulus and a flexible fiscal policy.

The potential for creating new jobs by using these three approaches is simply enormous. A great many capitalist and part-capitalist countries, perhaps most, fail to come close to their potential full-employment growth because they fail to properly manage total demand and/or structural competition. They suffer a lack of customers and a lack of jobs. This chapter and Chapter 5 will explore how that potential can be reached. We will start by examining the first requirement, limiting any outbreak of inflation by using monetary restraint to reduce demand.

Controlling Inflation by Controlling Demand

Since the awakening, excessive inflation has virtually always been met by monetary restraint. That restraint increased interest rates, slowed economic growth, and sometimes brought recession. Monetary restraint has a dual anti-inflation impact. It reduces total demand, and it also increases competition. But it is a special kind of competition. I call it *below-capacity* competition. As the economy slows, business firms have to compete more aggressively for orders. Workers have to compete more aggressively for jobs. Monetary restraint can be very effective in containing inflation, but the below-capacity competition is a product of undesirable (but necessary) slower growth and higher unemployment.

In the United States the Federal Reserve has been given the responsibility for limiting demand to control inflation. It has not always accepted that responsibility. It allowed inflation to accelerate beginning in the mid-1960s and to continue to accelerate, irregularly, until 1980, when the inflation was broken by aggressive monetary restraint that produced a deep recession (see Chart 4.1). We learned a great deal from that experience about how to handle bouts of inflation. First we learned the necessity of attacking inflation early before expectations of a continuation of accelerating prices sets in. Once expectations of continued inflation are established, accelerating wage gains become the norm. Business plans and labor contracts

Chart 4.1 Inflation Rate (CPI) and Civilian Unemployment Rate (Annual Data)

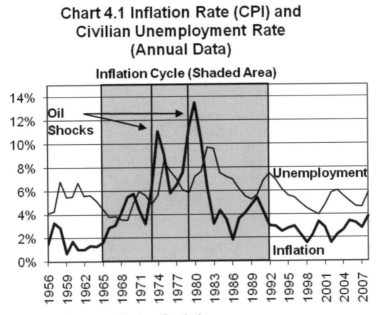

Source: Bureau of Labor Statistics

assume higher prices will follow. These inflationary expectations are hard to break.

After inflation began to accelerate in 1965, only halfhearted attempts were made to break it until 1981, when the inflation rate had already gone from 2 to 16 percent on a monthly basis. Restrictive monetary policy that produced intense below-capacity competition—more than 10 percent unemployment in the labor market and capacity utilization below 70 percent in the manufacturing sector—was required to break that inflation. The higher-than-average unemployment that prevailed *during* 5 years of the accelerating inflation together with the high unemployment necessary to *break* that inflation were the severe penalties suffered for allowing the inflation to develop. Even with that recession, the inflation rate, the interest rate, and the unemployment rate did not return to near normal until the mid-1990s.

The three-year intermittent recession from 1980 through 1982 was necessary shock treatment to break the inflation. It was engineered by application of very restrictive monetary policy under the leadership of newly appointed Federal Reserve chairman Paul Volcker. This action required great courage. Alan Greenspan acknowledged our debt to Mr. Volcker when he pointed out that Volcker had done the "heavy lifting" in the necessary task of inflation control.

The quarter century of much-improved economic performance since the "shock treatment" has demonstrated that we have indeed learned the need to attack incipient inflation early. Twice in that 25-year period, inflation began to accelerate—in 1989 and 1999. In each case money was tightened, and a mild recession occurred. But no shock treatment was required. In 1994, a tiny blip of inflation appeared. Slight monetary restraint brought a slowing of price increases with hardly a hint of recession. The Federal Reserve had learned.

But something even more important has been learned. Besides learning to act promptly we have learned *what to do* to control inflation. If you doubt that we have learned a lot about inflation control, go back and read the monetary debates of the late 1960s and 1970s. Those debates were a mass of confusion and indecision. Whether to use fiscal or monetary restraint, how soon to act, what economic indicators to follow, and how frequently to intervene were some of the questions debated. No consensus came close to being achieved. The contrast between that confusion and today's generally accepted monetary views is as the difference between night and day. We still have some differences about inflation control. But the Federal Reserve now clearly bears the responsibility to fine-tune the economy, and it uses short-term interest rates as the most obvious (but not the only) measure of monetary accommodation. The improved economic performance of the last two decades is testimony to what we have learned. But we can't stop now. We still have much to learn in order to create the kind of economy we should have and some day will achieve.

As this is written in early 2009 it appears we are in a recession caused by a massive failure of subprime mortgages. It was *not* caused by accelerating over-all inflation that had to be slowed. This subprime mortgage debacle represents a major learning failure. We failed to *maintain the quality of credit* in our financial system. Many failures to maintain the quality of credit in the past have led to serious financial difficulties. We should have learned. As described in the following chapter, we almost certainly will learn this time.

Something must be said about the oil shocks. Many people believe that the oil shocks were the cause of the 1970s inflation. But as Chart 4.1 shows, the inflation cycle began in 1965, eight years before the first oil shock. The inflation rate was far advanced by that time. The second oil shock came in late 1979 just prior to the peak of the inflation cycle. The oil shocks exacerbated inflation but certainly did not cause it.

Maintaining Very Full Employment by Improving Structural Competition

Writing these next several pages has been a delight. To describe how many governments, during the period of awakening, learned how to bring inflation under much better control is indeed a pleasure. And it is doubly satisfying to realize that these governments did it largely in the right ways. They gained better control over their budgets and monetary policies to reduce excessive aggregate demand, as discussed above. But more important, they increased the intensity of structural competition so that extensive use of below-

Chart 4.2 Advanced Economy Inflation Rate (Consumer Prices)

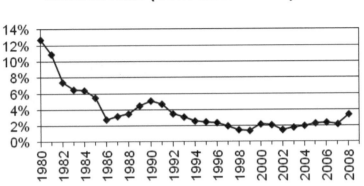

Source: International Monetary Fund

capacity competition with rising unemployment and slowing growth was not as often required. Improvements in structural competition are not by any means complete, but the expanding intergovernmental competition to attract capital investment, as described in Chapters 2 and 3, will likely keep it improving.

Chart 4.2 shows the decline in the combined inflation rates of *advanced* countries from 1980 to the mid-1990s and the rough stabilization around 2 percent since that time. *Developing* countries didn't begin to break accelerating inflation until the early 1990s.

This section describes four of the policies that governments used to achieve the exceptional improvement in structural competition. It also points out why the four policies will not likely be reversed, and how they can be further improved. These four policies are: opening borders to greater imports; opening to foreign direct and portfolio investment; deregulating economic activity; and restraining business and labor monopolies.

Opening Borders to Greater Imports

Anyone who doubts that the governments of the world have learned much about how to manage structural competition should examine Chart 4.3. In the last half century, governments have opened their borders to imports, increasing those imports to an average of nearly 27 percent of GDP—a growing percentage of a growing GDP. Open borders are evidenced by nonweighted average tariff barriers in developing countries declining about two-thirds to just over 10 percent since the beginning of the awakening. (The large rise in imports after 1972 was due to the sharp rise in oil prices. Oil is a major part of total imports.)

After World War II several advanced-country economists had encouraged developing countries to adopt an *import substitution* program. They had argued that the developing countries could not compete on world markets so they should close their borders to many imports and produce their needs locally. Of course this resulted in inefficient local monopolies and relatively stagnant economies. Governments have learned a lot about the need for international competition since that time.

Opening borders to substantial imports is absolutely essential to a well-functioning competitive capitalist economy, but it is no trivial or easy accomplishment. It is usually difficult because increasing imports often brings unpopular job losses to some domestic industries. The connection between rising imports and rising exports is often not appreciated by the general public. The fact that governments have overcome the difficulties and opened borders to greater imports shows that they have learned much about the needs of capitalism.

Chart 4.3 World Imports of Goods and Services (% of GDP)

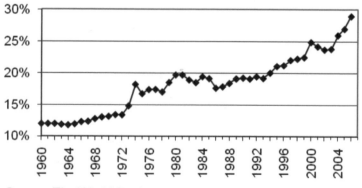

Source: The World Bank

International trade has long been justified on the grounds of *efficiency*. Each country specializes in what it does best, making for efficient production. But the *increased intensity of competition* in each country is an equally important justification for free trade. Increasing the *number of sellers* in an industry keeps competition rigorous, holding prices down and increasing jobs by requiring less price-restraining below-capacity competition. Most countries have a long way to go to complete this learning process. There is still opportunity for greater international competition, which would reduce even further the need for below-capacity competition and, in turn, speed job creation.

Opening Countries to Direct and Portfolio Investment

At the end of World War II many developing countries had a vivid memory of colonialism. They resolved not to be dominated again by foreigners. So they protected a number of industries by preventing foreign companies from buying existing companies, from starting new companies, or even from buying shares of stock in existing companies. Most governments have since learned better. They see foreign companies building plants in other countries,

Chart 4.4 World Foreign Direct Investment, Net Inflows (% of GDP)

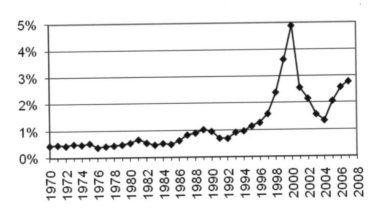

Sources: The World Bank, IMF, and UNCTAD

51

creating jobs, and they want a share of the action. Now most governments are trying to improve their economic environments to make them more conducive to attracting capital investment. This change in policy represents a powerful burst of learning and, as Chapters 2 and 3 described, will have a wonderfully beneficial impact on twenty-first century development.

Chart 4.4 shows world foreign direct investment as a percentage of GDP. It will decline in the current recession but after that will grow strongly. Nearly all the stars will be in alignment to produce a long-lasting surge in such investment, increasing competition even more. Consider the following trends:

• Companies, especially in advanced countries, will have large amounts of investment capital, and access to much more. They will be searching for places to invest it to produce the growth that stockholders demand.

• Companies will go abroad for a wide range of reasons, including the search for cheap labor, raw materials, markets, and technology.

• The *risk* of foreign investment has diminished since the end of the Cold War. More governments are now recognizing that legal protection of private property is necessary to attract capital investment. It was not long ago that fear of government expropriation kept many companies from investing abroad.

• Foreign investment is now in fashion.

• Opening borders to *imports* is the quickest way to get competition in a country's domestic manufacturing, agriculture, and mining industries. Opening borders to *direct foreign investment* goes much farther, bringing stronger competition to retail, wholesale, construction, public utility, and other industries. Altogether the opening of borders to imports and investment is the surest way to increase inflation-inhibiting competition, allowing the use of aggressive monetary and fiscal policy stimulation to maintain full employment.

When the United States reduces barriers to imports or when U.S. companies close factories to move production abroad, some American workers lose their jobs. Lives are disrupted. This downside to increased international trade must not be ignored. It becomes very painful when alternate jobs are not available. The fear of job losses tends to weaken support for expanded international trade. That is why a flexible fiscal stimulus plan to shorten recessions (described in Chapter 5) and Herculean efforts to maintain intense inflation-restraining structural competition (as described in this chapter) are so important.

The United States has gone a long way toward improving the availability of jobs. Since the beginning of the awakening, imports have grown from about 10 percent of GDP to about 18 percent today. And yet, the unemployment rate has not risen. It has actually declined from just under 6 percent in 1979, the year before the 1980 recession started, to about 5 percent before the current recession began. Most of those who lost jobs because of increased imports have found other jobs, perhaps not quickly enough or as high-paying a job, but they are not all unemployed.

Deregulating Economic Activity

Many countries around the world have shed socialist-type regulation, freeing up entrepreneurial opportunities and incentives. This deregulation has been part of the learning process of that 20-year period of awakening that is changing the world so much. Deregulation has occurred in part-capitalist and mostly-capitalist countries as well as in some fully socialist countries.

The roots of socialist doctrine extend deep into the past. The first large-scale experiment began with the communist revolution in Russia following World War I. The second major experiment accompanied the arrival of communism in China in World War II. The worldwide Great Depression in the 1930s convinced much of the world that capitalism had failed. Socialist planning and controls were widely adopted in countries that were partly or largely capitalist.

India provides a vivid example of the stagnating impact of socialist doctrine. One reads the record of India's economic performance with a mixture of sadness and hope. Sadness comes from an awareness of the immense human suffering produced by the stubborn efforts to make socialist planning and control work for four decades after Indian independence. Hope springs from an awareness of the enormous positive impact that recent deregulation and future deregulation can have on jobs and living standards in that vast country that will soon have the world's largest population.

At independence in 1947, India was saddled with Gandhian economic ideology. A desire for economic self-sufficiency kept borders largely closed to imports and to foreign investment. A fetish for small-scale production kept India from adopting much modern technology. Productivity stagnated. A distrust of the market and overconfidence in the ability of government to manage the minutia of production and trade led to the "license raj," a complex maze of licensing, regulation, and red tape that was required to do business in India.

The reforms of 1991 abolished industrial licensing with several exceptions. Entry requirements (including limits on equity participation) for foreign direct investment were relaxed. Private investments were allowed into sectors such as power, which had been reserved for public sector investment only.

India's remarkable efforts to liberalize industrial policy were equaled by efforts to liberalize its trade policy. Tariffs were sharply reduced. In addition to tariff restrictions, a myriad of nontariff barriers including import licensing, quota restrictions, a highly overvalued rupee, and strict limits on foreign ownership and investment had severely limited India's global economic involvement. Those restrictions have been modified.

India's "mini-revolution" beginning in 1991 is a work in progress. Liberalization has been only partial. Deregulation still has a long way to go. But competition with next-door China will keep reform alive, and the capitalist century will likely see India joining the ranks of prosperous, dynamic world leaders.

India is an extreme example of government regulation hampering entrepreneurial initiatives and weakening structural competition. Many other governments have also been struggling to break free from the worst of their regulations. Europe particularly has troubles with regulation of its labor markets. Most countries have opportunities to improve structural competition by deregulation. This is not to imply that all regulations are bad. Some, like those that preserve the integrity and stability of the banking system, are essential. But those that clearly weaken structural competition bring with them the penalties of inflation, central bank restraint, unemployment, and slow growth.

Restraining Business and Labor Monopolies

In a well-functioning market economy, wages paid by each company are just high enough to attract and retain qualified workers, and profits are just high enough to attract investment capital. Any device such as a labor union or a business combination that boosts wages or profits (and correspondingly, prices) above those levels generates inflation, central bank restraint, and job losses. Since wages (and benefits) make up half to two-thirds of the cost of doing business, they are of critical importance.

Little change in labor *legislation* has been made in the United States in the last several years, yet labor union membership has declined sharply from 20.1 percent of total employment in 1983 to 12 percent in 2008. The decline has come entirely in the private sector. Public sector union membership has remained stagnant. The decline in union membership in the private sector has almost certainly been a result of international competition. Unions in the private sector can deliver above-market wages to their members only when employers have sufficient market power to pass the wage increase on to the consumer in higher prices. International competition has limited that market power of employers. Consequently, union power to increase wages has diminished, and the attractiveness of labor union membership has also declined.

The U.S. automobile industry is an example of an industry that for many years had sufficient market power to grant wages (and benefits) far above those necessary to attract qualified workers. Market power enabled companies to pass those wage increases on to the consumer in higher prices. But then foreign competition increased. Market power diminished. Auto companies still have high union-induced legacy health-care costs, pension costs, and wages, but they can no longer pass these unwarranted costs on to the consumer. The impact, therefore, is loss of sales and loss of jobs. International competition has been a major factor in the ability of the United States to restrain prices and wages without the use of extensive below-capacity competition with its accompanying unemployment and slow growth.

A major opportunity is still available to improve competition and restrain inflation: changing the method of wage determination under union bargaining. When unions are involved, wages are set largely by the *infliction of misery* standard. That is, the power of the union to increase wages depends largely on the union's ability and willingness to inflict misery on the employer, a city, a region, a school district, or the whole country.

The 2005 transit worker strike in New York City at Christmastime is an example of a public-sector union holding a great city hostage at a critical time to preserve employee benefits and gain increased wages. Wages and benefits were already above those necessary to attract qualified workers. Many other New Yorkers would have loved to have those transit worker jobs. Any wage and benefit increases must be paid by increased taxes or by increased fees for riders. At some time in the future (after a few decades of further learning about inflation and its causes), people will wonder why the United States ever tolerated the "infliction of misery" standard as a determinant of fair wages. New Yorkers may already be wondering.

The 2002 labor dispute between the West Coast International Longshore and Warehouse Union and the terminal operators represented by the Pacific Maritime Association provides a private-sector example of a union gaining substantial contract improvements by inflicting massive misery on employers, workers in related industries, stores, and many other individuals and companies in need of import or export services. The International Longshore and Warehouse Union controls most of the port labor on the West Coast—loaders, unloaders, and everyone else who moves cargo to or from ships. When it was unable to get a contract that met its desires, the union cut productivity nearly in half by a work slowdown. The Pacific Maritime Association responded with a lockout, costing the overall economy over two billion dollars a day, until President Bush finally ended the lockout by executive order. Wage and benefit increases were not necessary to attract and retain workers. Workers were already extremely well paid. The average earnings for full-time longshoremen working 2,000 hours a year were $123,464. Foremen made about $192,000. When the Port of Los Angeles needed to fill 3,000 jobs in August 2004, more than 300,000 people applied for the positions, which were awarded by lottery. Any wage above the amount necessary to attract qualified workers adds to costs and prices and brings the inflation rate a bit closer to the ceiling that calls for Federal Reserve restraint, a slower economy, and unemployment. The infliction of misery was very effective in achieving the union's goals.

Wages should not be determined by the ability of unions to inflict misery on the employer and the public. They should be just high enough to *attract and retain qualified workers*. The amount of that required wage should be determined objectively by examining past quit rates and numbers of job applicants that respond to normal recruiting practices. Labor law should insist that those facts be given paramount consideration in wage negotiations. That can be done through the Federal Mediation and Conciliation Service (FMCS).

The FMCS was established in 1947 as an independent agency of the United States government. The agency was given the mission of preventing or minimizing the impact of labor-management disputes on the free flow of commerce, by providing mediation, conciliation, and voluntary arbitration services. In effect it was designed to get contract settlements, not to determine the *terms* of the settlements. Government clearly has a responsibility to try to maintain peace in the labor market, but I suggest that it should also have the responsibility to try to reduce excessive wage settlements gained by the threat of infliction of misery. The FMCS should not dictate the terms of settlements. But it should make certain that the negotiators pay paramount attention to the proper standard of wage determination. Wages should be just high enough to attract and retain qualified workers. The FMCS should also make certain that the wage be determined by objective data including past quit rates and the number of applicants responding to ordinary recruitment practices. That data should also be made public. The public can understand this approach. They have important interests because wages affect the prices they pay and the tax burden they bear for municipal services.

Governments should use the "attraction and retention of workers" standard for setting wages in their own operations. And, of course, they should use quit rates and the number of applicants responding to ordinary recruitment practices to justify the wages necessary to attract and retain workers. Governments have many opportunities to use this approach in units such as the postal service and utilities like the New York City transit system.

Changing the standard for setting wages is *not* of minor importance. It has the possibility of achieving a significant reduction of the inflationary pressures that lead to unemployment. The impact of the infliction of misery standard of wage determination on wages, inflation, and unemployment is not measured *only* by successful strikes. The *threat* of such strikes also boosts wages above their economic justification.

Of course the ability and willingness to inflict misery is not the only factor in union wage determination. The employer cannot grant wage increases unless it has the market power to pass the wage on to the public in higher prices or to absorb it through improved productivity.

Unions often argue that high corporate profits justify higher wages. They say that the increased wages will come at the expense of excessive profits. That is rarely the case. Increased wages are largely passed on to the consumer, sometimes not immediately but over a short period. Furthermore, if the corporate profits in an industry are out of the reach of *potential* competition, they should be subject to better enforcement of antitrust laws, rather than being used as a justification for higher wages that will likely just increase prices and unemployment.

When corporations have sufficient market power to maintain profits above the amount necessary to attract capital investment, that market (monopoly) power is a job destroyer because it produces prices that are higher than necessary, adding to the inflation threat. Although total corporate profits are small compared to total wages and benefits, excessive profits are still an inflation threat. Competition in the corporate sector must be diligently protected by antitrust enforcement.

Corporate profits fluctuate substantially, rising and falling with the ebb and flow of business activity, but their proportion of national income over the long term has been reasonably steady. In 2005 corporations received almost exactly the same percentage of national income as they did in 1959—12.4 percent. Both of those years were years of substantial prosperity. Individual industries often achieve high profits for a short period, but those high profits usually attract competition that drives the profits down. Sometimes, of course, it takes too long for that competition to develop. Price-fixing agreements among sellers, when allowed to prevail, are especially pernicious in keeping prices high. The antitrust laws have been reasonably effective in policing those agreements.

Benefits of Improved Structural Competition

Throughout the 1965-1980 period of accelerating inflation, the Federal Reserve was reluctant to use aggressive monetary restraint to bring inflation under control for fear it would slow growth and increase unemployment. But in the subsequent 20-year period of awakening, the Federal Reserve's improved monetary policy stabilized the inflation rate in the United States. It did so without causing a deep recession like the recession of 1980-82 needed to break the inflation. U.S. performance was matched by many other countries. *The better performance would not have been possible without the inflation-restraining intensification of structural competition as has been described in this chapter.*

Chart 4.5 shows the advanced economies' unemployment rate, which actually *declined* during that period when inflation was brought under control in contrast to the previous period of

Chart 4.5 Advanced Economies Unemployment Rate

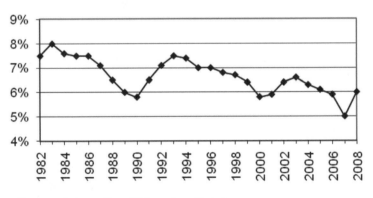

Source: International Monetary Fund

accelerating inflation when unemployment rose. Stronger structural competition made strong below-capacity competition, characterized by a slow-growing economy, unnecessary. The current recession in the United States beginning in 2008 was not caused by the necessity to curb inflation. As Chapter 5 explains, it was caused by failure to maintain the quality of credit in the banking system.

Unemployment also fell in emerging markets and developing countries. Unemployment data are not available for emerging market economies, but Chart 4.6 shows the acceleration of the growth rate of GDP for emerging markets and developing countries, which could not have occurred if unemployment had been rising.

Chart 4.6 Annual Percentage Change in Inflation-Adjusted GDP for Emerging Markets and Developing Countries

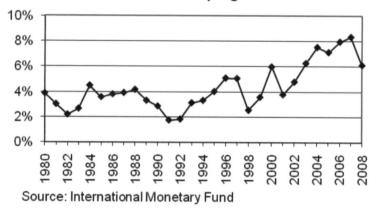

Source: International Monetary Fund

One other beneficial characteristic of that period of awakening must be considered—productivity. Chart 4.7 shows the productivity growth rate for nonfinancial corporations in the United States. Productivity improvement slowed during the period from 1965 to 1980 when inflation was accelerating. It improved after 1980 when the inflation rate was slowing. The inverse relationship between changes in the productivity growth rate and changes in the inflation rate is not coincidental. *They are both products of the changing intensity of competition,* a relationship we will now explore.

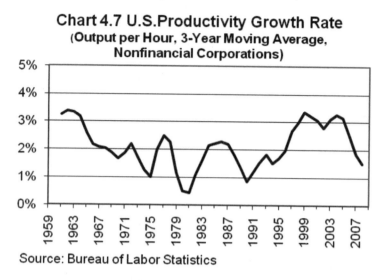

Chart 4.7 U.S.Productivity Growth Rate
(Output per Hour, 3-Year Moving Average,
Nonfinancial Corporations)

Source: Bureau of Labor Statistics

Competition, Inflation, and Productivity

The intensity of competition is not a constant. It varies widely over long periods and often rapidly over short periods. The great importance of the changing intensity of competition requires that efforts be made to measure it, predict it, and *manage* it. We will consider only long-term changes in productivity.

Structural competition, the intensity of competition built into the structure of the economy, covers every aspect of the economy that affects the ability of competition to hold prices down. International competition and effective antitrust laws clearly enhance the effectiveness of structural competition. But so do education, a well-functioning capital market, an efficient tax system, a fair and just legal system, a culture of tolerance, and many other factors that provide incentives and opportunity to engage in productive economic activity. These *positive* factors result in a large number of efficient producers, which makes for more competition. On the *negative* side, clearly monopolies in business and labor, excessive taxation, and cost-enhancing government regulation limit the ability of competition to hold prices down. All these factors (both positive and negative) operate mainly on the *supply* side of markets.

Chart 4.8 shows a fairly reliable *inverse* relationship between the inflation rate and the productivity growth rate. Analysts have spent considerable effort trying to determine whether changes in inflation drive changes in productivity growth or vice versa. Results have not been conclusive but suggest that changes in the inflation rate may more often be the driving force. I take a different view, but it is compatible with that conclusion. I believe that both variables are driven in large part by a third factor, the *changing intensity of competition*.

Chart 4.8 Changes in the CPI and Business Productivity, Three-Year Moving Averages

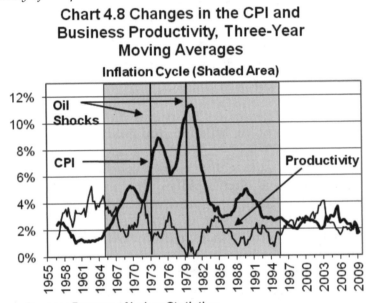

Source: Bureau of Labor Statistics

It is not hard to believe that the inflation rate is an inverse approximation of the intensity of competition in an economy, rising rapidly when competition is weak and remaining low when competition is strong. It is also believable that productivity improves rapidly under the stimulus of strong competition and remains lethargic when competition is weak. Therefore, prices and productivity show a reasonably reliable *inverse* relationship. They both reflect the changing intensity of competition, but in different directions.

We must have strong competition to restrain inflation and to improve productivity. The new, more reliable Federal Reserve policy of restraining inflation with tight monetary policy coupled with the maintenance of intense structural competition will likely insure that *both* the low inflation rate and a relatively high productivity growth rate will extend far into the future.

Could the Trend Toward More Intense Structural Competition Be Reversed?

Much of the agriculture industry, many businesses, and most labor unions quite understandably try to gain favorable legislation that will insulate them from competition. Labor unions have the most comprehensive list of new programs, which, if adopted, would seriously weaken structural competition. That wish list includes new legislation that would guarantee stronger union bargaining power and greater ability to organize new members. These expanded powers would certainly weaken structural competition. Union opposition to free trade agreements would, if enacted into law, limit foreign competition. Any social benefits to be provided by *employers* would add to the cost of doing business and thus raise prices.

Now suppose some administration in Washington announced it would enact a substantial part of the union wish list, not just a token adjustment but meaningful changes in the law. Bond and stock markets are very sensitive to threats of inflation. Wall Street analysts would likely sound the inflation alarm. Bond and stock markets would decline, threatening recession, and the proposed legislation would likely be modified or abandoned. The new, more reliable Federal Reserve inflation-control policy gives the security markets some restraining power on actions that clearly threaten to increase inflation.

A strong reaction by Wall Street analysts would likely appear in the event of *major* legislative proposals but would not likely arise in the event of minor changes even though they eat away at the foundation of structural competition. An insidious danger lurks in the legislative process. Structural competition has frequently been weakened by legislation because the side effects of that legislation on the ability of competition to restrain inflation were not considered when the legislation was designed. Consequently the impairment of the inflation-restraining power of competition has come as an *unintended by-product of scores of legislative initiatives.* It is time that the effect of legislation on structural competition receives equal billing and sometimes top billing when important legislation is considered.

The word "cost" must take on an expanded meaning in legislative design. Cost gets great attention now when it relates to government expenditures. It must be expanded to cover all *compliance* costs that get passed on to the consumer in higher prices. These costs are job destroyers. They bring us closer to the inflation ceiling that precipitates Federal Reserve restrictive policy with its slow growth and unemployment.

In coming years Congress will face hundreds of decisions where the impact on structural competition should receive consideration. Demands for social services, needs for alternative energy sources, global warming, infrastructure requirements—all these coming problems, and more, will require painful decisions. If several of these decisions hamper the ability of structural competition to restrain inflation, they will push the inflation rate above the ceiling that will require monetary restraint with its adverse side effects.

Chapter 5

SOLVING CAPITALISM'S
INSTABILITY PROBLEMS, PART 2

Financial panics accompanied by high unemployment have plagued capitalism almost from its beginning, creating damaging instability. Many of those panics have resulted from the issuance of large volumes of defective credit. Credit is defective when the probability is substantial that it will not be repaid when due. It is especially defective when it is granted in such quantity that defaults have a significant negative impact on the economy. The current subprime mortgage episode has involved massive amounts of defective credit that had little chance of being repaid. When defaults came in volume they had a drastic negative impact on the economy. To prevent financial panics we must learn how to protect the *quality of credit*.

The subprime mortgage crisis demonstrated two facts regarding what we have learned from previous crises arising from bouts of defective credit. First, it demonstrated clearly that we had failed miserably to learn the necessity of maintaining a high quality of credit in our financial system to prevent financial crises. Failure to learn was not limited to a few people in government. It included the Federal Reserve, government authorities involved with housing, Congress, the managers of Freddie Mac and Fannie Mae, the bond credit rating services, and hundreds of financial executives in large banks and other institutions who "invested" hundreds of billions of other people's money in subprime-mortgage-related securities.

But the subprime mortgage crisis also demonstrated that we have learned a great deal about *how to react* to a financial crisis. After 1929 we responded to the financial crisis by raising interest rates and taxes, thereby slowing the economy. Then we nearly destroyed international trade by raising tariffs. These actions turned a financial crisis into the Great Depression. In contrast, we reacted to the subprime mortgage crisis with extensive Federal Reserve and Treasury actions to flood the financial system with funds. We lowered interest rates. We took a number of steps to prevent a wave of bank failures. But we still have not learned how to take *quick and sufficient* steps to shore up consumer spending. More about this later.

The Quality of Mortgage Credit

The tale of the subprime mortgage debacle with its deteriorating credit quality has been told many times. But one element of that tale has rarely been properly explained. *Why did the quality of mortgage credit deteriorate so much beginning in the late 1990s?* Government pressure forced banks to find borrowers in low-income areas to expand home ownership to low-income families. To do this they had to lower credit standards, and Fannie Mae and Freddie Mac were content to go along with this policy. As credit standards were lowered and were found to be profitable, lenders were tempted to adopt even lower standards. In addition, Fannie and Freddie were allowed to vastly expand the amount of mortgages they could underwrite on the basis of their capitalization. The subprime mortgage boom was on its way. When writers discuss the question of *why* the subprime mortgage crisis developed, government *deregulation* based on ideology is often found to have been the culprit. This explanation is not quite correct. The *initial* cause of the subprime mortgage crisis was a well-meaning but badly designed attempt to expand home ownership to low-income families. The initial profitability of these mortgages led to weaker and weaker credit standards with escalating risks. New regulations should have been adopted to prevent that deterioration of credit standards. Perhaps ideology stood in the way of such expanded regulation.

The *mechanics* of the subprime mortgage debacle are now well understood. Thousands of banks and mortgage companies loaned money to people on mortgages that could not come close to meeting traditional lending standards. They had low teaser interest rates that reset upward, sometimes automatically, sometimes when the market rate of interest rose. Loans were often made without careful checks of the information provided by the borrower, or even without getting an accurate appraisal of the value of the home. These mortgage loans were usually sold to Fannie Mae or Freddie Mac, two privately owned giants, and then bundled to serve as collateral for bonds. These bonds were sold to banks and others throughout the world. The repayment of the bonds had the appearance of being insured through a new device called credit default swaps. The "insurers" backing these bonds did not have the reserves necessary to guarantee their repayment. As strange as it may seem, the bonds were given AAA ratings by the bond rating agencies. Many bonds were bought because of the AAA rating and also because of the erroneous assumption that the United States government was backing the bonds. That assumption was made because they were issued by Fannie Mae and Freddie Mac, which were originally sponsored by the United States government.

Trillions of dollars of these defective loans became part of the foundation of our money and banking system. These loans helped fuel the housing price bubble. But it could not last. When housing prices stopped rising and defaults began to appear, the bond insurance failed, and the house of cards built on the foundation of defective credit collapsed.

It has not been a pretty sight. Hundreds of thousands of foreclosures have demonstrated the mistaken judgments of both borrowers and lenders. Many of those who have lost their homes were just speculating on future increases in home prices. But some were trapped by those hard-to-justify mortgages with low initial teaser rates. Total damage to the economy cannot yet be determined, but without financial intervention by the Federal Reserve and support to banks and consumers by the Treasury, a crushing recession could follow. However, *with* that intervention, we have a reasonable probability of escaping with a manageable recession.

We will surely regard this subprime mortgage episode as a learning experience. We will likely come out of it with a far better system to preserve the quality of mortgage credit. In most aspects of commerce in a capitalist economy, presumption should be against government regulation of markets unless extraordinary conditions prevail. But in the financial sector, unregulated competition seems to drive lenders to take greater and greater risks to increase returns. Judgment is often warped. Presumptions against regulation of the quality of credit in the financial sector are not strong. Certainly the belief that the financial system can be self-regulating has received a fatal blow.

The Home Price Bubble

Should efforts have been made to prevent increasing home prices from surging into a bubble? If so, how? Some economists argue that the Federal Reserve should have raised interest rates earlier. But we had not yet recovered to full employment, and *expectations* of accelerating inflation in the broad economy were not serious. Could we have raised interest rates enough to stop the bubble from escalating without seriously slowing the total economy? Probably not. And slowing the economy would have been a heavy and unnecessary price to pay. A better approach would have been to control the *quality* of mortgage credit—by setting more rigorous standards on the quality of mortgages that Fannie and Freddie could purchase. That would have slowed the rise in home prices.

Some observers had argued that our complex system of securitizing mortgage loans and selling them to investors worldwide was shifting risks to institutional investors better able to appraise and bear those risks. The record indicates that that was not true. Our financial system had become so complex with off-balance-sheet liabilities, credit-default swaps, and other devices that few could recognize the magnitude of the risks involved. They did not pay sufficient attention to the deteriorating quality of the underlying mortgage loans. No doubt this complexity will be limited by better bank regulation. The system must be made more understandable so that the degree of risk can be estimated.

Alan Greenspan recognized the deterioration in the quality of mortgage credit and the increased risk but was willing to accept that risk to achieve wider home ownership. He wrote in *The Age of Turbulence*: "Of the nearly $3 trillion of home mortgage originations in 2006, a fifth were subprime and another fifth were so-called Alt-A mortgages. The latter are mortgages taken out by people with good credit histories, but whose monthly payments are often interest-only, and whose documentation with respect to the borrower's income and other characteristics is inadequate. Poor performance of this two-fifths of originations has induced a significant tightening of credit availability, with a noticeable impact on home sales. I was aware that the loosening of mortgage credit terms for subprime borrowers increased financial risk, and that subsidized home ownership initiatives distort market outcomes. But I believed then, as now, that the benefits of broadened home ownership are worth the risk. Protection of property rights, so critical to a market economy, requires a critical mass of owners to sustain political support" (p. 233).

Would not simple regulation of the quality of the mortgage loans at the time of origination have been desirable for both borrowers and lenders, and helped to better maintain full employment while still extending mortgages to those who could afford them? Surely reducing the demand for homes from subprime and Alt-A borrowers would have done much to curb the speculative home price bubble. It would also have reduced the magnitude of the credit crunch that followed. A better way must be found to extend home ownership to low-income families.

The Quality of Stock Market Credit

Could better control of the quality of stock market credit have significantly tempered speculation in the stock market bubble beginning in the late 1990s and thereby have reduced the depth of the subsequent recession? The risk of default was not the problem with excessive stock market credit. The problem arose because stock market credit aggravated stock speculation, and the subsequent collapse of the stock market bubble had an adverse effect on the economy. Of course, this adverse effect on the economy was far less serious than the adverse effect of subprime mortgages.

The Federal Reserve has been given the responsibility for controlling stock market credit and the tools for doing so. In 1934 Congress, smarting from the human devastation caused by the Great Depression, gave the responsibility for controlling *excessive* use of stock market credit to the Board of Governors of the Federal Reserve System. Excessive speculation in the late 1920s, financed by credit, was believed to have been a significant cause of the Depression. The Securities and Exchange Act stated: "For the purpose of preventing the excessive use of credit for the purchase and carrying of securities, the Board of Governors of the Federal Reserve System shall, prior to October 1, 1934, and from time to time thereafter, prescribe rules and regulations with respect to the amount of credit that may be initially extended and subsequently maintained on any security." An important note: The mandate was *not to regulate stock prices in general* but to limit the excessive use of credit and presumably thereby limit excessive speculation. The Federal Reserve tried twice to get Congress to remove that responsibility—in 1985 and 1995. Each time Congress refused. How should the Federal Reserve exercise this mandate?

For 30 years, from the end of World War II in 1945 to 1974, the Federal Reserve used changes in margin requirements to control excessive growth of margin credit. A margin requirement is the amount of cash (or other assets) that the investor must deposit to purchase a security. A margin requirement of 50 percent means that an investor can borrow only 50 percent of the purchase price of a stock. There were seven episodes of tightening. After 1974, this policy was abandoned. The margin requirement was left at 50 percent, where it stands today. That 30-year use of margin requirements was sufficiently successful to warrant its occasional use in the future. Only a tiny fraction of all stocks are bought on credit, perhaps fewer than 1 percent. But a far larger proportion of *speculative* purchases are made on credit and can be discouraged by aggressive increases in margin requirements. Raising margin requirements tends to dampen the speculative mood in the market.

The first five of the seven episodes of margin tightening, from 1945 to 1965, can be judged to have been successful (see Chart 5.1). First, they stopped the growth of margin credit quickly. Second, they apparently helped prevent the development of excessive speculation as judged by the fact that subsequent declines in stock prices were very small. The last two of the seven tightening episodes, in 1967-69 and in 1971-73, were *not* successful, for two reasons: margin restraint was applied only after margin credit had grown dramatically, and even then restraint was only weakly applied. The failure of the Federal Reserve to act promptly and vigorously apparently allowed serious speculation to develop, as judged by the sharp subsequent declines in stock prices—29 percent after 1968 and 43 percent after 1972.

When margin credit is rising rapidly and speculative froth is evident at a time when *general upward pressure on the Consumer Price Index is substantial*, the policy decision is clear. The Federal Reserve should increase interest rates to slow the whole economy to restrain inflation. The growth of margin credit will automatically slow as a by-product of controlling inflation. Such action should have been taken in 1967-68. But when margin credit and frothy stock speculation are rising at a time when consumer prices are steady, slowing the whole economy is an unnecessary and expensive option. That's the time when margin requirements should be used aggressively to help take the speculative froth out of the market.

Chart 5.1 S&P 500 and Margin Loans

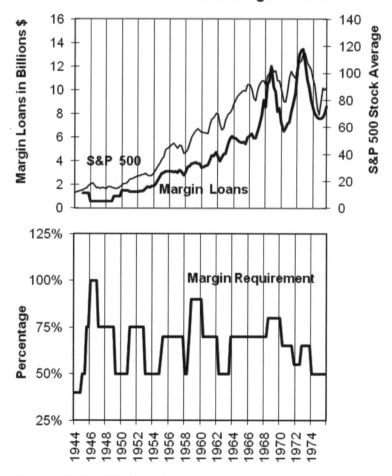

Source: Federal Reserve Board

One such occasion arose in 1997. The Federal Reserve governors had to make a difficult decision. As Chairman Greenspan describes the situation, they feared that a rapidly rising stock market *might develop* into a speculative bubble causing inflationary instability. To forestall such an eventuality, the Federal Reserve raised short-term interest rates by one quarter of a percentage point to 5.5 percent. The announcement of the increase indicated that it was done to address underlying forces that threatened to create inflation. Not a word was said about dampening speculation on rising stock prices. After an initial small drop, the stock market continued its surge—for three more years with substantial speculative froth. And as Greenspan says, "We never tried to rein in stock prices again." Note that the Federal Reserve was judging its lack of success by its *failure to curb stock prices* in general as measured by stock averages, *not by the lack of impact on margin credit and speculative froth*. The Federal Reserve does *not* have a mandate to control stock prices in general. It does have a mandate to control excessive use of credit. At that time, Greenspan did not mention the possible use of margin restraint, the tool explicitly given by Congress to control excessive use of credit and presumably excessive speculation.

The next two and a half years to the end of the millennium were a clear-cut stock market bubble with frothy speculation and rapidly rising margin credit. General inflation picked up only slightly and that increase was thanks largely to a small, temporary rise in oil prices. Unemployment dropped to 4 percent. All seemed well, except for that frothy speculation in stock prices. Perhaps aggressive control of margin credit would have limited the speculation of those last three years, thereby limiting the decline of the following three years in both the stock market and the general economy. Nothing would have been lost by raising those margin restraints to 100 percent.

Using margin controls today must seem to many like an old-fashioned, ineffective way to limit excessive speculation in view of the many computer-driven plans for speculation using many types of derivatives and leveraged funds. But after the current financial crisis is over, many of those recent speculative vehicles will be modified by legislation to protect the quality of credit and the transparency of the financial system. Margin controls may again become a useful vehicle to achieve Congress's long-ignored mandate to limit excessive margin credit and presumably speculation.

Flexible Fiscal Stimulus to Help Keep Recessions Mild

Two facts should guide the drafting of fiscal-stimulus legislation. First, we cannot know with confidence how much stimulus will be needed. Therefore, part of the stimulus package should be flexible, adjustable quarter-by-quarter as the economy changes and as our forecasts prove to be wrong. Second, the package must be strong enough at the outset to change early-recession gloom into a conviction that the stimulus will work. That conviction will come only if the stimulus starts strong and promises to change quarter-by-quarter to adjust for mistaken forecasts and changing needs, whatever they might be. A strong start with the assurance that stimulus will continue as needed until recovery is well under way *will likely require less total stimulus spending (and therefore less of an increase in the deficit)* over the span of the recession than a weak start, and a recession that drags on and on.

How Long and Deep Will This Recession Be?

At the beginning of 2009, a dark cloud of pessimism hangs over the United States as evidenced by, among other things, stocks selling far below the prices warranted by their latent earning power. Many people are saying that the current recession will be *more difficult to correct* than any economic decline since the Great Depression. That is not true. The intermittent recession of 1980-82 was far more difficult to correct because *inflation was rampant and had to be contained.* Remember, inflation is caused by too much spending in relation to the ability of existing competition to control prices. Therefore, to contain inflation in that early '80s recession, it was necessary to reduce spending by restrictive monetary policy. Inflation prevented the use of stimulative monetary and fiscal policy. By mid-1982, two-and-a-half years after the onset of that intermittent recession, monetary policy was still strongly restrictive with Treasury notes yielding about 14 percent. Core inflation was still at an excessive 6 percent, although down substantially from its high of 15 percent. In contrast, at the beginning of 2009, core inflation is less than 1 percent, having dropped from a relatively mild 3 percent. We do not have to restrain spending or monetary stimulus to curb existing inflation, and that gives us far greater freedom to bring the recession to an end by aggressive monetary and fiscal stimulus.

Yet, two factors are now worse than in 1980-82. The banking system is much weaker. The Federal Reserve and the Treasury have taken unprecedented steps to rescue the banks. They have not yet been fully successful, but they will continue their efforts until they succeed. Also, the bursting of the home-price bubble and the sharp decline in stock prices have made people feel much poorer. Stimulating consumer spending will be more difficult. These two factors call for bold stimulus in contrast to the inflation of 1980-82 that limited the use of stimulus.

With aggressive fiscal policy to supplement aggressive monetary policy already in place, we should be able to keep the current recession milder than that of 1980-82. Millions of unemployed workers demand it. But if we don't act boldly, unemployment could top the 11 percent peak reached in 1982. In 1980-82, high inflation required restraint in using fiscal stimulation. *Today, any failure to use aggressive fiscal stimulation must be considered a policy mistake.*

The frailty of our banking system is now well known, but the problems that would follow a sharp rise in the savings rate are not as well recognized. Chart 5.2 shows the personal savings rate in the United States. For over 30 years prior to 1992, that rate stayed mostly above 7 percent. It then declined irregularly until 2004. For three years it averaged approximately 0.5 percent. Recently, it has started moving up. That decade-long decline in the savings rate (increase in consumer spending) was a major support of total spending and business activity.

Much of the decline in the savings rate has been attributed to the boom in asset prices—first the stock market and then home prices. Homeowners felt more wealthy, encouraging them to spend more and save less. Even more important than that general feeling of growing affluence was the practice of using home equity as a kind of bank account. The Federal Reserve has estimated that consumers withdrew spendable cash in large amounts based on the

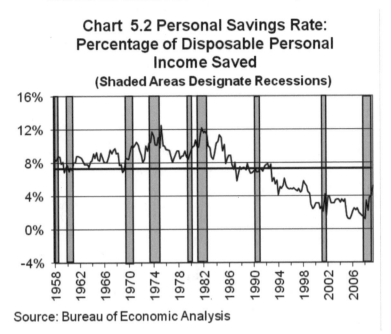

**Chart 5.2 Personal Savings Rate:
Percentage of Disposable Personal
Income Saved**
(Shaded Areas Designate Recessions)

Source: Bureau of Economic Analysis

appreciated value of their homes by assuming bigger mortgages, home-equity loans, and other techniques—up to six percent or more of personal disposable income. That amounts to more than half a trillion dollars each year for the past few years. Part of that money was undoubtedly spent on consumer goods and accounts for part or all of the declining savings rate.

Just as the housing-price bubble reduced personal saving, the bursting of the bubble will likely increase personal saving. How much, we don't know, but it could be very large. A return of the savings rate to the 7-to-10 percent range that prevailed so long would reduce consumer spending by more than 700 billion dollars. Together with its effect on other spending, that decline would require a huge amount of government fiscal stimulus. We must be prepared for a wide range of possible needs and be able to change plans quickly when conditions warrant or our forecasts are proven wrong. We must have a plan that is adjustable on a quarter-by-quarter basis.

In summary, the frailty of our banking system and the likelihood of a major increase in the savings rate indicate that the present recession could be long and deep unless offset by major government spending or tax reductions. Furthermore the absence of serious inflation gives us the latitude to use extremely aggressive fiscal stimulation to supplement aggressive monetary stimulus already in place. We cannot afford timidity.

Infrastructure Spending

Just because the stimulus package as a *whole* must be flexible does not mean that *all parts* of the package must be flexible. At present, we badly need a great deal of infrastructure spending. Most infrastructure spending is slow to start. Nevertheless, it can be used as a stimulus *if flexible spending is used to offset the spending shortfall until infrastructure spending kicks in.*

Forecasting the need for fiscal stimulation is extremely difficult, but that does not mean we should not try. A likely major increase in the savings rate and the weak capital position of the banking system will probably require significant fiscal stimulation for two or more years. Therefore, fairly long-term infrastructure spending projects can be used as long as they are clearly needed, and as long as legislators realize that if the infrastructure spending continues after the economy recovers and the danger of an overheating economy appears, taxes will have to be raised to cover those continuing expenditures. Authorization of necessary infrastructure spending should be made with emphasis on projects that can be started quickly, and can be completed within a year or two. But any project will qualify as long as legislators recognize the need to raise taxes to cover expenditures that last too long.

The Flexible Part of the Stimulus Package

Attempts were made in 2001 and 2008 to stimulate consumer spending by sending tax rebate checks to consumers. In 2001, the Treasury mailed $300 checks to individuals and $600 to married couples. The total rebate amounted to $38 billion, or 0.4 percent of GDP. In 2008, the Treasury mailed checks of $300 to $600 to individuals and $600 to $1200 to married couples, plus an additional $300 per child. The total rebate amounted to about $100 billion.

A survey made in 2001 at the time the checks were mailed indicated that only about 20 percent of consumers "mostly spent" their rebates. The remainder was "mostly saved" or "used to pay down debt." Survey results were the same in 2008 as they were in 2001.[6] However, another economic study, published in the *American Economic Review*, found that over the six months following the mailing of rebate checks in 2001, consumer spending increased by approximately two-thirds of the amount of the rebate.[7] An economic study made in 2008 indicates that rebate checks increased nondurable consumption by 2.4 percent in the second quarter of 2008 and by 4.1 percent in the third quarter.[8] One might expect that the initial response to receipt of the checks would be different than the action taken over the following three to six months. As these and other studies indicate, consumers who initially paid down credit-card debt will often build it up again. Someone who deposited the check in a bank will often spend it in the following months.

The 2009 approach to stimulating consumer spending is different. A $250 payment is being made to each of the elderly, and the withholding tax is being temporarily reduced over the course of two years to provide a $400 increase ($800 for a married couple) in take-home pay to workers. This approach does not meet the requirement of a prompt and substantial consumer stimulus. Some experts argue that dispensing the money a little bit at a time will ensure that consumers spend it. It will be such a small addition to each paycheck that they will not notice it enough to use it for savings or paying down debt. This may be true, but a tax refund that is too small and gradual for consumers to notice is also too small and gradual to change their expectations or to restore confidence in the economy. Current forecasts (early 2009) indicate that we will likely suffer a deep and long-lasting recession unless we have a quick and aggressive government stimulus. Therefore, we need strong, *immediate* consumer stimulus, adjustable on a quarter-by-quarter basis as needs become evident. But it must also slow or stop when infrastructure spending rises and the economy is well on the way to recovery.

We need a program that will put a substantial amount of money into the hands of consumers immediately, together with the promise that additional quarterly payments will be forthcoming *as needed* until infrastructure spending expands and the economy recovers. Since this flexible stimulus plan must be adjustable on a quarter-by-quarter basis, authority must be given to the president to determine— within specified limits—the amount needed for each quarter. That authority has built-in controls. The president would be anxious to end the stimulus program to make room for permanent spending projects or tax cuts. Also, excessive stimulus that threatened to overheat the economy would bring a Federal Reserve rebuke in the form of unpopular increases in interest rates.

Who would receive the stimulus checks? The government has a number of mailing lists it can use, including Social Security for the elderly, and withholding and payroll-tax rolls for workers. Increased payments could also be made to the unemployed. Experts who are familiar with these programs could work out appropriate lists of people who should receive stimulus checks.

This program should be aggressive. Early, aggressive stimulus of the economy would likely require less *total* government spending (a smaller increase in the deficit) than weaker spending which allows the recession to drag on and on *with anemic tax receipts to the government*. We cannot afford timidity.

Conclusion

The largest United States' recession since World War II, the intermittent recession of 1980-82, was caused mainly by the failure of the Federal Reserve to attack inflation early, allowing inflation habits and expectations to become so ingrained that they were hard to break. I believe we have learned from that mistake. It will not likely be repeated.

Our current recession was caused by a financial system that indulged in wild and irresponsible risk-taking not regulated by government. I do not believe we will ever again fall victim to the notion that the financial system can be trusted to regulate itself. In essence, I believe that we have learned from our mistakes.

We cannot eliminate recessions, but we can learn to keep them mild and infrequent by appropriate monetary and fiscal policies and by better management of the quality of credit as described in this chapter. We must keep trying.

Chapter 6

WHEN CAPITALISM MEETS THE WORLD

As capitalism spreads around the world, it faces Herculean challenges from authoritarian governments, corrupt governments, failed states, festering animosities, rigid religious certainties, terrorism, and most of all—ignorance. But the new, more stable capitalism is expanding rapidly, overcoming obstacles. This chapter will explore briefly how the three powerful forces— the lure of capitalist abundance, competition to attract capital investment, and the need for much wider trading areas—are faring as capitalism meets its adversaries in different regions of the world. World peace and prosperity are the prizes that capitalism can be expected to deliver.

China

Utter failure of China's communist system combined with the lure of capitalist abundance led Deng Xiaoping to start China on the road to capitalism in 1978. At that time China was dirt poor, lethargic, gray in appearance. There was a deadening sameness. Everyone wore Mao jackets. They rode bicycles or walked. The landscape was dotted with half-finished, apparently abandoned structures that were monuments to the socialist inability to plan projects that were within their capability to complete. And China was boring, dreadfully boring. For example, in one city the most exciting event seemed to be the spectacle of international tourists walking from an arriving plane to the terminal building. Chinese turned out in throngs to line the path to watch this simple tourist procession.

China's progress since then has been spectacular. It has captured the imagination of the world. For 30 years it has maintained a growth of output fairly close to 10 percent. It now has per-capita output of about $7,000. (All per-capita output figures used in this chapter are based on purchasing power parity, taken from the 2008 Index of Economic Freedom by the Heritage Foundation.) That is about a quarter of the per-capita output of Japan and each of the major European countries. China's success is important to the world. By successful example, it has strengthened the lure of capitalist abundance to other governments. To intensify the attraction of that abundance we need to have it on display in all regions, in all cultures, and in countries of all sizes. China, the world's most populous country, has by its success told governments that big countries can make rapid progress toward that abundance much like those small Asian neighbors (South Korea, Taiwan, Hong Kong, and Singapore) that began their moves to capitalist abundance many years earlier. India, the other Asian giant, is following. Its mini-revolution started in 1991, much later than China's.

Will China stay on course? Three factors that are emphasized throughout this book indicate that it will.

First, *China's ability to attract foreign capital investment*. Chapters 2 and 3 argued that to attract capital and achieve capitalist abundance, countries must provide a favorable investment environment, including a rule of law to protect private property and the primacy of contract. This investment environment must include those features required to make possible an effective market-managed economy. Although in many ways China's investment environment is still deficient, it has been adequate to attract large amounts of foreign direct investment. In 2006 China received about $80 billion of foreign direct investment. This was far more than any other developing country received. However, in relation to the size of its total output and its population it was not nearly as impressive. Nevertheless, China has put in place the investment structure that has attracted many corporations from various countries to build facilities there. They must believe that the favorable investment environment will last and improve. That is an encouraging vote for China's future progress. Receiving foreign direct investment is valuable in itself, but making the changes in the political-economic structure that are necessary to attract that investment is even more important. That is why foreign direct investment is one of the important indicators of a country's fundamental progress toward a successful capitalism.

Second, *the ability to contain inflation while maintaining rapid growth and full employment*. This book has argued repeatedly that two features are necessary to maintain full employment—adequate demand in the market to initiate economic activity and intense competition built into the structure of the economy to channel that demand into production rather than into inflation. Governments can generally increase demand by monetary and fiscal policy without too much difficulty. However, they often find the maintenance of intense structural competition both painful and difficult. But China has accomplished both. That long-term growth record has been accomplished with little inflation. In 1993-94, a spike in inflation caused mainly by a rise in food prices was attacked early and brought under control without seriously harming the growth rate. As this is written in early 2009, China is facing another modest inflation thanks partly to the rise in food and fuel prices but also partly to excessive expansion policies. It will also likely be brought under control without doing long-term damage to the growth rate. Being able to simultaneously maintain growth and low inflation for so long is a great accomplishment.

A low inflation rate accompanying rapid growth is valuable in and of itself, but making the adjustments to the economy required to gain the structural competition necessary to maintain low inflation is even more important. That is why the existence of low inflation along with a rapid growth rate is another valuable indicator of the fundamental soundness of an economy.

Third, *growing integration with the world*. Another repeated argument of this book is that the huge variety of products now available requires very wide trading areas, certainly international in scope. Countries that do not establish those wide trading areas will not be able to achieve a substantial degree of capitalist abundance. China has established those trading areas. In 2006 China had exports plus imports amounting to an astonishing 78 percent of GDP. That number is distorted by a large volume of imported parts and materials that are re-exported after further processing. But still, there is no doubt that China has integrated itself with much of the world and is therefore highly interdependent with the rest of the world. Many people in the United States consider China an enemy and fear that one day extensive military conflict will break out. That seems unlikely considering the collapse it would cause in supplies of necessary goods, and the loss of markets on which many Chinese depend for jobs.

81

In summary, China has created a political-economic structure that has
- attracted substantial amounts of foreign direct investment,
- contained inflation while maintaining rapid growth, and
- integrated itself into a large international trading area.

Any economy that can do that probably has a political-economic system that will achieve a highly successful capitalism. Yet China has many serious problems. The growing number of civilian protests against government action is a sure sign that all is not well. The number of government-acknowledged protests has skyrocketed from about 10,000 a year in the mid 1990s to around 100,000 in recent years. They are also getting larger. Some protests number more than 100,000 demonstrators. Although a few protestors have been killed, most of them have not been met with Tiananmen Square-type brutality. Most protests are in rural areas against local governments.

By adopting one single reform, China could sharply reduce civilian protests, reduce corruption in local governments, jump-start China's rural economy, vastly improve the efficiency of China's agriculture, and take another step toward capitalism and democracy. In China the right of peasants to farm a piece of land is maintained only by dint of possession, or by an unreliable, nonrenewable lease. The farmer cannot sell the land or borrow against it. That rural land has become a source of corruption for local government officials. When land is needed for commercial, industrial, or civic development it is simply taken by local officials with minimal payment to the farmer. It is then transferred to developers but with a substantial profit retained by those local officials. No wonder the civilian protests have been rising.

Now suppose that China's government decreed that farmers be granted deeds that represent full ownership of the land, including the right to sell it and borrow against it. A market would quickly develop for the land, establishing objective prices that local governments would have to pay when appropriating it for any purpose. This would help satisfy farmers and reduce corruption of local officials. Farmers selling the land would receive capital, some of which could be used to start the thousands of small businesses needed by a thriving capitalism. The consolidation of farms would improve the efficiency of agriculture. The average household farm is less than an acre. It would be a win-win program. China has recently taken steps to strengthen private property rights, but much is left to be done, especially in rural areas.

Will China's government move to more civil liberties and greater democracy as *all* advanced capitalist countries have done when they changed from government-managed economies to capitalism? We cannot be certain, but the forces for such a movement as described in Chapter 3 are strong. One country, Singapore, a small but highly successful capitalist country, is a partial exception to the pattern of other advanced capitalist countries. Singapore's civil liberties do not come up to the standard of, say, the United Kingdom, but most liberties are honored *except when they impinge on the ability of the People's Action Party to maintain control of government*. And even Singapore's civil liberties and democracy are far superior to those of noncapitalist countries.

Will China's leaders succumb to arrogance and overconfidence? Historian Herbert J. Muller, looking back at the many governments that he had studied, concluded: "Nothing fails like success." He was referring to the tendency of governments to become arrogant and overconfident when they have had a substantial run of success. Failure often follows. Invasions of Russia by Napoleon and Hitler are prime examples. Could failure resulting from arrogance and overconfidence follow China's remarkable achievements?

China's leaders will certainly make mistakes due to overconfidence as have American presidents and leaders of other advanced countries. But they are not likely to make the most serious mistake, military aggression to acquire land and control of the people that work the land. As Chapter 3 argues, rivalries among today's governments to outperform in achieving wealth, power, and prestige find an outlet in increasing productivity rather than in the military acquisition of territory. The result today is usually cooperation among governments rather than military aggression. Of course, that little spot of land called Taiwan carries immense historical baggage that could be troublesome. But relations between China and Taiwan seem to be improving, and interdependence is growing. The power of economic forces to build greater interdependence and cooperation among countries is a major theme of this book. That interdependence will likely preclude serious military adventures arising from any overconfidence and arrogance that infect China's leaders.

The Asian Capitalist Contagion

China is now in the spotlight. But it is only one of the nearly 15 Asian countries that have responded to the lure of capitalist abundance and are actively moving toward capitalism. Most of these countries have improved their investment environments to be able to receive substantial foreign direct investment. Many of them have kept a fair degree of price stability along with growing economies. And most of them are integrating their economies into wide trading areas. These three improvements are strong indicators that their basic economies are developing toward a successful capitalism.

The fact that these 15 countries are spread out widely on the road to capitalism provides another reason for optimism. The younger capitalists are learning from both the successful policies and the mistaken policies of the more advanced capitalists. Developing Asian countries have annual outputs ranging from that of Old Japan and the four Asian tigers that have annual per-capita output near $30,000, down to Pakistan and Bangladesh with per-capita output of around $2,000. These varied Asian countries are competing with one another to attract capital investment and in other ways, but they are also cooperating with one another. They are negotiating regional trade agreements that open borders, increase vital competition among their producers, and improve efficiency. Every one of those Asian countries has much to learn about capitalism, but they are learning. Competition will drive that learning process.

In 100 years, maybe within as few as 50 years, Asia should be a prosperous, peaceful, capitalist continent containing half the population of the world. Together with North America, Europe, and most of South America, that should establish a powerful anchor for world peace. (Central Asia is not included in these projections. In several ways it is more like the Middle East.)

Russia

Russia's recent military incursion into Georgia has raised fears that Russia will attempt to acquire by military means part of its empire lost when the Soviet Union collapsed. Also, Mr. Putin's recent overriding of some private property rights has raised questions about the future of investment in Russia. These are serious worries, but the stock, credit, foreign exchange, and other markets will likely force Mr. Putin back onto the path toward capitalism and peace fairly soon.

For a decade after the breakup of the Soviet Union, Russia's political-economic system was in turmoil and was not generally considered to be sufficiently attractive to bring in large quantities of foreign direct investment. However, that perception changed in the last few years as Russia stabilized. The quantity of foreign direct investment rose substantially. Also, portfolio investment grew, as indicated by the rapid rise of Russia's stock markets, and Russian corporations borrowed heavily on the world credit markets. But after the Georgia military incursion, Russia's stock markets dropped sharply, far more than those of most other developing countries in the worldwide financial panic. Foreign direct investment will likely also decline, and credit will be hard for Russia's companies to obtain on international markets. The ruble will be weak on the foreign exchange market. These international markets will educate Mr. Putin as to the need to reestablish the perception of a Russian future that includes peace and the rights of private property. Mr. Putin will likely learn soon as Russia's economy falters and the need to attract capital investment grows. Of course, any significant increase in the price of oil would help a little to strengthen Russia's position.

The competition built into the structure of Russia's economic system has been inadequate to hold prices down when the economy grows rapidly. That is a serious weakness that will likely take time to correct. Adequate structural competition is extremely important but often difficult to achieve.

Russia's ability to integrate into a wide international trading area has been damaged by its military adventure. Russia has been trying to get into the World Trade Organization for more than a decade. Gaining entrance to the WTO with all its advantages will likely be postponed. A much-needed regional trade agreement with Europe may also have to wait. A large trading area is mandatory for Russia. That need may help redirect Mr. Putin's policies.

Russia is a moderate-sized country with a population of about 140 million, less than half the size of the United States. Its population is declining. It has annual per-capita output of about $11,000, not much more than a quarter of that of the United States, one third that of the major European countries, and somewhat less than that of some eastern European countries formerly within the Russian orbit.

Several Central and Eastern European countries that were formerly within the Soviet orbit have been growing rapidly and doing so without the vast oil and gas resources that have spurred Russia's growth. In 2006 that European area received more than twice the foreign direct investment that Russia received. Eastern Europe is clearly becoming integrated into a wide, productive trading area. If Russia continues its course of military intimidation and weakening of private property rights, Eastern Europe on Russia's western border and China on its southeastern border will rapidly pull ahead in the competition to achieve capitalist abundance. That will not go unnoticed by the Russian population that yearns for capitalist abundance. Although Eastern Europe, like most of the world, has been hurt by the recession, it appears to already have in place much of the basic structure that will make possible recovery and renewed growth.

Driven by the need to attract capital investment, both foreign and domestic, Mr. Putin will likely begin strengthening the protection of investment provided by a reliable rule of law, and will moderate his belligerence. Russia will move more convincingly along the road toward a genuine capitalism.

South America

South America has not had great success with either capitalism or democracy. Chile began a successful shift toward capitalism a few years prior to that period of awakening. But Chile is a small country. Its example was not followed. Governments in South

America have frequently been stalled on the path to capitalism by corruption, a monopoly culture, excessive populism, and failure to control inflation until it gets out of hand. The future of capitalism in South America depends mainly on Brazil because it is so large compared to the other countries.

For several years beginning in the mid-1980s, Brazil suffered an *annual* inflation rate of more than 500 percent, a clear example of irresponsible government. In the last decade, that average inflation rate was brought down to the mid-single digits. That was a superb achievement. It was done by more responsible monetary and fiscal policy, opening borders to imports, privatizing state enterprises, and making social services and other government functions more fair and efficient. That is standard procedure for developing an effective capitalist economy. Brazil appears to be ready to lead South America to a prosperous capitalism.

Venezuela is moving away from capitalism. It is already in trouble as a result of inflation. It would be in *deep* trouble if it were not for its huge oil reserves. Rising oil prices have provided the income to make possible its move to a less-efficient economic system. This chapter will describe how we can prevent the rising demand for oil from giving Venezuela and other oil-producing countries the ability to neglect the requirements of capitalism that lead to prosperity and freedom.

Sub-Saharan Africa

The immediate outlook for Sub-Saharan Africa is not bright. It has been, and still is, plagued by disease—HIV, malaria, and others. It has been wracked by many small wars, mostly civil wars. Its governments have given in to all of the temptations that impede the progress to a prosperous capitalism, especially corruption.

Botswana has for some time demonstrated the ability to achieve a fairly prosperous capitalism. With a population of less than 2 million, it is not large enough to command sufficient attention to serve as an example, and it, too, bears the HIV affliction.

But a brighter future lies ahead for Africa. Demand for African natural resources is increasing and will continue to increase. Furthermore, one should not overlook South Africa. Its economic performance has been good but not spectacular. It is improving both by speeding its growth rate and slowing inflation. Its elimination of apartheid without serious bloodshed was a great achievement.

Looking farther ahead, a larger force for development will come into play. Right now, many developing countries around the world can offer *cheap labor* to attract capital investment. But as wages in those countries (largely in Asia) rise, companies in today's advanced countries and in those rapidly developing Asian countries will be looking for new sources of cheap labor. Then, far more corporate executives will be roaming around Africa looking for investment opportunities. Africa's growth rate will accelerate.

The Middle East: Capitalism's Greatest Challenge

Can capitalism turn today's fractious Middle East together with its environs into a large, dynamic, peaceful, prosperous, cooperative area based on a predominant Muslim culture with the holy cities of Mecca and Medina at its center? Could religious faith become sufficiently relaxed and the Middle East become so thoroughly integrated with the rest of the world that it becomes an attractive place for non-Muslims to visit, work, set up businesses, and live? Could tolerance become so ingrained that even memories of the stoning to death of women and the beheading of apostates will fade away as have memories of the burning at the stake of heretics in Europe and the witchcraft trials in America? Capitalism's task will be hard and the struggle long. But it has already begun.

It's a puzzle! How long will it take capitalism to work its magic on the Middle East? Three *long-term major* problems have combined with a number of short-term problems (that may become long-term major problems) to create that puzzle. Oil, the Israeli-Palestinian conflict, and extreme Islamist teachings are the three long-term major problems.

Oil has created a serious difficulty. Several countries have so much of it, and it has become so valuable, that those countries have been given a *reprieve* from the necessity of making all those fundamental changes necessary to attract capital investment, both foreign and domestic, in order to gain capitalist abundance. That reprieve is not permanent, but some governments, basking in the glow of sudden wealth, are acting as though it is.

The *Israeli-Palestinian conflict* is the second major long-term problem. That problem has festered for more than half a century. It is virulent. It shows up as enmity everywhere in Arab countries and to some extent throughout the 1.3 billion Muslim population. Among Arabs, *humiliation* is an important part of that enmity. Arabs have lost four wars, decisively, to Israel. A desire to regain self-respect is not a minor motivation. The enmity arising from the conflict will not be quickly ended.

Extreme Islamist teachings, the third major problem, have gained a foothold among various groups throughout much of the Muslim world, although their influence appears to be declining in a few countries. These teachings come in a variety of forms. The most extreme call for Islamist law, Islamist courts, and Islamist governments to replace civil law, courts, and governments. Interpretation of Islamist law is generally harsh, rigid, and often violent.

Extremist Muslims are at present apparently immune to that powerful force that is driving the rest of the world—the necessity of creating an environment that will attract capital investment in order to gain capitalist abundance and freedom. These extremists have never had a real opportunity to see capitalist abundance in a Muslim culture. As that abundance finally comes on display in several Muslim countries, the extremist view will likely fade.

Extremist Muslim groups have an audacious goal—to take control of some of the world's governments. If they succeed in any country, as the Taliban did in Afghanistan in connection with the end of the Soviet occupation, the government-managed economy will fail and serve as a useful bad example to the rest of the world. That is, unless they take control of a major oil-rich country. Then, a government-managed economy could survive a long time and do great damage before it fails.

What a contrast the Middle East is to Asia where competition among governments to attract capital investment is driving governments rapidly toward capitalism and eventually to democracy. The Middle East was the cradle of civilization. Irony would be served if that area were to be one of the last regions on earth to receive the full civilizing benefits of a *mature* capitalism.

A *long-term* solution to Middle Eastern turmoil will require three successful projects: settle the Israeli-Palestinian conflict, find new energy sources that will reduce the tyranny of oil, and neutralize extremist Muslim teachings. The first project is far beyond the scope of this book. The problem of extremist Muslim teachings will be approached later in this chapter, but we must now examine ways to reduce the ability of oil exporters to flout the normal requirements needed to attract capital investment as described in Chapters 2 and 3. Reduction of the power of oil exporters will require the development of alternate energy sources.

The Importance of Finding New Energy Sources

Three intertwined energy problems are driving the United States and the world to the development of new sources of energy:

• *Growing dependence on oil* makes the world vulnerable to the instability in the Middle East where a large proportion of the world's oil reserves are concentrated. A sudden decline in supplies from that area could create serious problems worldwide.

• *The rapid growth in demand for energy by developing countries* will put upward pressure on the price of oil. Increased oil revenues to oil producers will enable them to resist pressure to adopt the policies that are necessary to attract capital investment and that are favorable to capitalism and freedom. Russia and Venezuela are included along with the Middle Eastern countries. Furthermore, increased oil prices will intensify inflation, making the maintenance of full employment more difficult. Any recession-induced decline in the demand for oil will not last long in the face of the growing demand from developing countries.

• *Global warming*, with drastic consequences, is more and more being recognized as an imminent danger.

All three of these problems call for a single solution. We must reduce our dependence on fossil fuels, and we must do so with a sense of urgency.

Governments have taken several steps to slow the growth in demand for fossil fuels. They have subsidized wind and solar power, and some energy research projects. They have set some energy-efficiency standards, especially for cars. They are beginning to modify some of the roadblocks to the use of nuclear power. This is a piecemeal approach. Most of these changes involve government attempts to pick winning technologies, something governments have not done too well in the past. This approach has probably been appropriate to jump-start the necessary changes in production and use of energy. But it has been a little like trying to drive a railroad spike with a tack hammer. If the polar ice caps shrink, glaciers continue to melt, hurricanes intensify, droughts become more severe, oceans rise, and more and more scientists argue that global warming is man-made, threatening imminent disasters, we will likely reach for a sledge hammer to drive that spike. It should be a carbon tax, a tax on all fuels determined by the amount of carbon dioxide (or its equivalent) released into the atmosphere.

A carbon tax, if enacted, should, as much as possible, be made revenue and inflation neutral. Making it revenue neutral means that it would not increase the *total* tax burden on the public. Inflation neutral means it would not add to inflationary pressures that would force the Federal Reserve to slow the economy by tightening money. A carbon tax to be effective would raise a huge amount of money until the use of carbon-dioxide-producing fuels declined. Reductions in sales taxes and payroll taxes could offset that tax. These taxes are borne by the broad public, as the carbon tax would be. Sales taxes are levied by state and local governments. Carbon tax revenues could be distributed to those governments in exchange for reduction of the sales taxes. We would pay *much more* for energy that releases carbon dioxide into the atmosphere, and we would pay a bit less for the whole range of consumer goods that don't, both fuel and nonfuel.

With a carbon tax, consumers—not government—would decide where to conserve in the use of carbon-emitting energy. Consumers might buy smaller cars, drive less, insulate their homes, buy energy-efficient appliances, or find some other way to save money by conserving carbon-based energy with its rising prices. Their individual decisions would be based on the price of each product (including taxes) in relation to their judgment of its benefit in their personal lives. When making a purchase they would not have to worry about the unknown energy efficiency of the product. The price would already account for that efficiency. Also, business—not government—would decide which alternative fuels would have the best likelihood of being successful, and thus deserving of large research and development expenditures.

The carbon tax would be reflected in the prices of all products emitting carbon into the atmosphere. It would therefore be inflationary. That would be offset by reductions in the prices of goods that currently bear the cost of sales taxes and to a large extent payroll taxes. Prices of all items, carbon and noncarbon, would move toward their cost plus taxes. Demand for carbon products would decline, and demand for noncarbon products (both fuel and nonfuel) would rise.

The initial carbon tax should be moderate but still large enough to capture the attention of business and the general public. It must be a convincing declaration that we are embarking on a long-term move to an energy system with far fewer carbon emissions. The law would have large built-in escalators. This would enable consumers to make better plans when deciding whether to buy a fuel-efficient car, a motor home, or even an energy-saving lightbulb. But, more important, it would unleash a torrent of research and development on new processes and products that would be competitive with guaranteed higher future prices for carbon-emitting fuels. For example, it would say to the coal industry: If you go on as now, your industry will decline and perhaps disappear in the next 50 years. But if you develop a feasible system of carbon capture and storage, your industry will grow several times. The coal industry could provide 100 years of substantial energy independence without adding carbon dioxide to the atmosphere. Surely that message would bring substantial expenditures by the coal industry for development of carbon capture and storage.

In addition to the carbon tax, government must continue to be involved in the nuclear power industry because it is already heavily involved in the nuclear power industry. So far, government involvement has been mainly negative, putting up roadblocks to nuclear power through extensive permitting, location, and design requirements. As is well known, France has demonstrated that reasonably priced nuclear power can be produced safely in large quantities with existing technologies. America could adopt this system.

The validity of the man-made global warming thesis may not yet have been fully established, but it is building. When the consequences of a possible future event are likely to be dire, as in the case of global warming, remedial action should be taken even though we are not absolutely certain that the feared event will materialize. Also, we cannot overlook the added benefits of becoming more energy independent. And we cannot overlook the enormous benefits of encouraging the governments of the Middle East and other oil-producing countries to adopt policies that will enable them to attract capital investment instead of relying on their oil revenues.

The coming growth in demand for energy will be enormous. That demand is coming at us rapidly. No great vision is needed to recognize the impact of the 85 percent of the world's population now living in developing countries adopting rich-country lifestyles. If man-made global warming is an imminent danger and we do nothing about carbon emissions, we may face catastrophe. If we make great efforts to find alternate fuels but global warming is *not* a danger, we will have done that which we must eventually do anyway. Not much will be lost. We, our children, or our children's children must develop vast new sources of energy. We have little to lose by speeding that development.

Developing countries will initially be more concerned with reducing particulates, sulfur emissions, and other types of visible and health-damaging pollution than they will with reducing carbon emissions. Furthermore, we will find great difficulty in getting those countries to adopt policies to restrain carbon emissions as long as our *per-capita* emissions are so much greater than theirs. Therefore we can expect greater success in gaining global warming cooperation from developing countries by substantially *reducing* our per-capita carbon emissions. And, of course, finding new economically feasible sources of energy will be important for them as well as for us.

The Lure of Capitalist Abundance Meets the Middle East

The lure of capitalist abundance will eventually triumph over complacent governments, badly informed governments, authoritarian governments, despotic governments, oil-rich governments, and extremist Muslim teachings in the Middle East and everywhere. Most people and governments want that abundance badly. Let's look at its progress in the Middle East.

The Middle East, together with its Muslim environs, is usually considered to be the most dangerous place on earth. Will it be tamed reasonably soon by the lure of capitalist abundance? In spite of the Iraq war, the conflict between Israel and the Palestinians, the instability in Lebanon, Iran's nuclear ambition, the Taliban insurgency in Afghanistan, Sunni-Shia conflict, political instability in Pakistan, and extensive problems with Muslim extremists, the Middle East seems to be witnessing the birth of a genuine, though still fragile, capitalism. The Middle East has long been of a fractious nature. But something has happened in the last few years that should eventually bring a much-needed development to that region. That powerful "something" is cross-border investment and trade.

In the past few years, direct foreign investment has surged in some Middle Eastern countries. *When private capital investment begins to flow across borders, we must pay attention.* It may mean that governments have finally begun to recognize their responsibility for doing all those things necessary to achieve capitalist abundance by attracting capital investment. That would put them on course for further opening of borders to investment and trade, reducing restrictive government regulation, minimizing corruption, limiting the power of monopolies in business and labor, curbing excessive government spending, and educating the workforce. The benefits from just a few years of success could give them adequate incentives to keep their young and fragile economies on the road toward a genuine capitalism.

The lure of capitalist abundance will not impact all Middle Eastern governments equally. We must examine the countries individually to see how vigorously they will engage in the competition to attract capital investment in order to gain capitalist abundance.

Four Muslim countries with little or no oil production are situated along the west side of the Middle East. Three of them have recently experienced a strong surge of direct foreign investment—Turkey (generally considered part of Eastern

Europe), Egypt, and Jordan. All three have seen a growth rate accelerating into the 5-to-8 percent range. That is not quite a China growth rate but must be considered a substantial success. Syria, the fourth country, lags at a substandard 2.5 percent growth rate. Turkey, with a population of 70 million, has made a magnificent adjustment in recent years. It has brought inflation down from an annual average in excess of 50 percent to single digits while speeding its growth rate into the 6-to-8 percent range. Its performance was a result of better fiscal and monetary policy and its becoming more attractive to capital investment, both foreign and domestic. Turkey's inflation rate and output have suffered recently along with most of the world with the oil inflation and the onset of a world recession. Turkey now faces a test as to whether or not it has learned from its recent years of economic success.

Egypt has also moved to a more rapid growth rate, but its outlook is not as solid as Turkey's. In the World Bank's ranking of countries on the basis of ease of doing business there, Egypt ranks worse than average. But there are two bright spots. First, Egypt's overall score has begun to improve, and second, its score in trading across borders is well above average. That is a good omen for the future. Egypt has recently demonstrated its ability to attract substantial direct foreign investment and should be able to learn to reduce the barriers to developing domestic entrepreneurs. It has a reasonable chance of becoming an example of a rapidly growing *Muslim* capitalist country. And it is Arab. It has a population of about 75 million.

Jordan is also on the fast track. Its prospects are bright. But it is a small country, with only about 6 million people. Nevertheless, in the next 25 years it will likely become a third example of Muslim countries learning how to gain capitalist abundance. It, too, is Arab. Jordan, together with Turkey and Egypt, should provide a total population of about 155 million Muslims living in growing capitalist abundance on the western edge of the Middle East. That's half the population of the United States.

Syria, with a population of 20 million, has not yet reduced the barriers to free market activity enough to attract adequate foreign direct investment, but with nearby examples of improving capitalism in a Muslim culture, it, too, may join the ranks of rapidly growing Middle Eastern countries. The lure of capitalist abundance is strong. Pressure on Syria will be great to catch up with neighboring Turkey and Jordan.

Israel, a small country of about 7 million, also located on the west side of the Middle East, is now an advanced country with output per capita only moderately below the output of the major countries of Western Europe. But because of the many political, religious, and ethnic problems, it is not yet well integrated with most of its Muslim neighbors.

The small countries with large oil production along the eastern edge of the Arabian Peninsula provide a special group with excellent prospects—Kuwait, Bahrain, Qatar, United Arab Emirates, and Oman. Their total population comes to only about 12 million. They have a huge amount of *oil* abundance and a growing amount of *capitalist* abundance. They are prosperous, have high growth rates, and generally have free markets. They cannot serve as useful examples of *capitalist* abundance to countries with few oil resources, but they have served as useful examples to that large, oil-rich Saudi Arabia next door. They may yet serve as an example to oil-rich Iran, with which they have extensive trade.

Saudi Arabia, with a population of 24 million, basks in oil abundance. It is one of the world's largest producers. But even with its oil riches, it needs capitalism to provide jobs for its rapidly growing population. Its economic growth rate is only about 5 percent, and much of that represents the growing value of its oil production. Saudi Arabia ranks much better than average in the World Bank's appraisal of ease of doing business. It is solidly in the capitalist camp, but it is largely a defective state capitalism due to the heavy presence of government in the oil and related industries. To make it fit better into the rest of the world, Saudi Arabia has begun to rein in the powerful religious authorities that have kept its culture rigid, harsh, and unattractive to most of the world. It has also begun an extensive industrialization program in plastics, aluminum, steel, and other industries where it can take advantage of its large oil and gas reserves.

Much of Saudi Arabia's expansion has been based on inefficient development made possible by the immense income from oil. Its school system, though lavish, often fails to turn out graduates with useful skills. It has a bloated government sector, made that way to provide jobs for many of its young people who have few useful skills.

As Iraq stabilizes, it, too, will be a highly profitable oil producer with production in the neighborhood of 4 to 5 million barrels a day. It will have to call on the international oil companies to rebuild and expand its oil industry, so it will be largely in the capitalist camp. It may, however, start out as a defective state capitalism.

Iraq and Saudi Arabia in the heart of the Middle East will provide important markets of roughly 50 million people. They will have an immense source of capital from their oil revenues that can be invested in the region as its growth potential becomes evident.

Iran, on the eastern edge of the Middle East, has attracted little direct foreign investment since it turned more belligerent a few years ago. It has a growth rate of about 6 percent, much of which is accounted for by growth in the value of its oil production. Its oil abundance does not replace its need for capitalist abundance. Its annual per-capita output is only about $8,000, much of which is oil production. It fares badly in the World Bank's appraisal of the ease of doing domestic business. Until it improves its market environment and calms its belligerence, it will be unable to grow fast enough to provide jobs and goods to satisfy its rapidly growing population. Iran, sooner or later, with its population of 70 million, will be forced to follow the path of the other countries and learn how to attract capital investment, both foreign and domestic.

In summary, a potentially vigorous capitalism is beginning to come alive in the Muslim Middle East (including Turkey). The three sprouting capitalist countries along the western edge of the Middle East have a population of about 150 million. The rich oil producers of Saudi Arabia and the little countries along the Persian Gulf, soon to be joined by Iraq, have a population of about 60 million and an immense income from oil. That oil revenue is beginning to provide investment funds for the area and is providing a growing market for goods produced in the area. Laggard Iran will eventually succumb to the lure of capitalist abundance on display in growing splendor just off its western border. All together, the Middle East will likely become a vibrant center of improving capitalism in a

Muslim culture. Democracy has been late in coming to the Muslim Middle East because capitalism has been late in coming to the Muslim Middle East. A genuine capitalism is likely on its way. Genuine democracy will follow, but not until capitalism is more firmly established.

The Middle East has been badly fractured. Autocratic governments, jealous of one another, have been unwilling to cooperate adequately, even in wars with Israel. Sectarian differences, mainly Sunni and Shia, and various ethnic differences have exacerbated the fractured nature of that area. But under the pressures driving toward wider trading areas described in this book, those divisive forces may dim. With the many aspects of the Muslim culture common to most Mideast countries, and with the holy cities of Mecca and Medina at the center, Islam may finally become a unifying force. With growing trade and investment, the Middle East and its Muslim environs may finally become a twenty-first century, peaceful center of capitalist abundance in a Muslim culture.

But wait—we have not yet considered the Muslim extremists with their suicide bombers, difficult to protect against. The heart of the extremist movement is now along the border between Afghanistan and Pakistan, just beyond the eastern edge of the Middle East. Al Qaeda is headquartered in that mountainous area. Can the lure of capitalist abundance tame the extremists so isolated in the mountains? Not likely until the extremist insurgency is controlled by military force. For the United States and NATO to allow the Muslim extremists to regain control of Afghanistan is almost inconceivable. Now that the Iraq war is winding down, more attention will be paid to Afghanistan. A good deal of time may be required to stabilize the country, but the consequences of failure are so dire that we cannot allow it to happen.

In Pakistan, a large Muslim country of more than 160 million people, a struggle between Muslim extremism and capitalist abundance is under way. Since Pakistan has nuclear capabilities, victory by capitalist abundance is mandatory. Pakistan is a poor country. Its output per capita is less than a third of the per-capita output of Turkey and about two-thirds that of India. Pakistan was wounded at birth in 1956 when it separated from India. Turbulence developed as large numbers of Hindus moved from the new Pakistan to India and Muslims moved from India to the new Pakistan. Pakistan was born as twins—East Pakistan and West Pakistan, separated by great distance and different interests that generated conflict. They were finally partitioned when East Pakistan became Bangladesh in 1971. Pakistan's history has been marred by war, military takeovers of government, and poverty.

An interesting coincidence appears in the histories of Pakistan and China. At almost exactly the same time that Deng Xiaoping turned China toward capitalism in 1978, a military dictator, Zia ul-Haq, turned Pakistan toward greater emphasis on Islam. He dramatically expanded the construction of Madrassas (the religious schools) and increased the number of Mullahs. Since then Pakistan's growth has been sluggish and China's growth has been phenomenal.

But Pakistan is showing signs of awakening. It, too, has recently attracted sharp increases in direct foreign investment, and its growth rate has moved up to the 6-to-8 percent range, at least temporarily. Economic development is concentrated around Karachi in the south. Muslim extremism is concentrated in the mountainous northwest border with Afghanistan. The powerful lure of capitalist abundance should win in the battle against Muslim extremists as the people get an opportunity to make a clear choice between the two. Pakistan should receive support from both advanced capitalist countries and moderate Muslims everywhere.

This view of the Middle East and its environs will seem overly optimistic to many, but it is based on a strong conviction that the power of capitalist abundance can replicate capitalism around the world. And the growing number of capitalist (and would-be capitalist) governments is creating a dynamic competition to attract capital investment. Under that competition, governments will learn to adopt the policies that will create prosperity, peace, and democracy. The Middle East is not immune to these forces. But for now military force is required to keep the extremists from expanding their base.

Those three driving forces—the lure of capitalist abundance, competition among governments to attract capital investment, and the need for wide trading areas—will create a thriving capitalism of half a billion population in the fractious Middle East and its environs. Whether or not that thriving capitalism in a Muslim culture is achieved in 50, 100, or 150 years will depend largely on how soon governments recognize the need for school systems that turn out students qualified to meet the needs of a productive capitalism.

Chapter 7

CAN THE UNITED STATES COMPETE?

The United States is today the world's lone superpower. It will not long bear that distinction. What will change it? Capitalism! Capitalism will not reduce America's power, but it will increase the power of several other countries that are shifting away from government-managed economies. The world will have a few *major* powers, but no superpower. The world will also have a large number of small powers that will be important because they will act as blocs. Not a single American should mourn the coming loss of the superpower designation. The new world order will be far more peaceful and prosperous.

The Nature and Source of National Power

Military power has long been the major form of national power. The United States military is far stronger than that of any other country. We spend about as much on the military as the rest of the world combined. Military power will continue to be of prime importance for many years, but will gradually be supplemented (and eventually surpassed) by other forms of power. As international trade and investment expand, the countries of the world will become more interdependent and peaceful. As nations devote more of their energies to acquiring capitalist abundance, they will become more prosperous and stable.

Wealth will continue to be an important source of power. It commands respect, envy, and imitation. As argued in Chapters 2 and 3, the lure of capitalist abundance is dramatically changing the world by enticing governments to turn to capitalism. That is evidence of massive power.

In the capitalist century, *prestige* will be a growing part of national power. It, too, will command respect, envy, and imitation, but not as quickly or as reliably as wealth. People have widely divergent views as to what features command prestige. I suggest that "quality of life" measures such as freedom, civil liberties, education, protection of the environment, health, longevity, absence of crime, tolerance, and low incidence of poverty will be in the ascendency as measures of prestige. Indeed, quality of life covers everything that can be included in the goals that America adopted at its inception—life, liberty, and the pursuit of happiness. Achieving these goals while retaining the productivity and dynamic nature of capitalism will be a challenge.

Productivity is clearly the major source of national power. It makes possible large expenditures on the military. It provides the capitalist abundance that is changing the world. It makes possible the space spectaculars, remarkable inventions, tall buildings, great universities, and impressive museums that build prestige. It provides the means for substantial social services so vital in a modern economy, something the humanitarian-oriented socialists could never do because socialism was not productive.

Competition Between Economic Systems

For nearly half a century after World War II, government-managed socialism was locked in a crucial conflict with market-managed capitalism. That competition between economic systems was a significant part of the Cold War. The United States and western Europe were the main champions of capitalism. The Soviet Union and China, together with their many satellites, supported socialism. Three specific rivalries prevailed within that broad competition, almost as if they were deliberately designed to test the effectiveness of the two economic systems: East Germany vs. West Germany, North Korea vs. South Korea, and mainland China vs. Taiwan. The capitalist victory was overwhelming.

When socialism collapsed in the Soviet Union and China, the view that capitalism would soon dominate the world became conventional wisdom in many quarters. Countries around the globe, both developed and developing, reduced government control of their economies, leading to the remarkable growth in the world economy that we experienced. It is almost inconceivable that any country that has tasted a significant amount of capitalist abundance and freedom of choice would return to a full socialism with government ownership of most of the means of production and employing most of the nation's workers. But we are now entering a new long-term competition between two economic systems—capitalism and *state* capitalism.

In both these systems a majority of productive assets are under private ownership and management. However, state capitalism has a larger proportion of state ownership than capitalism. State capitalism interferes much more in the market mechanism by regulations such as price controls. Countries such as China that have been creeping out of socialism are still strongly state capitalists and in some cases are actually adding to their regulatory controls.

In coming years, comparisons will constantly be made between the overall performance of countries with varying degrees of *state* capitalism and those with more complete capitalist systems. A competition between the various types of capitalism is developing. But a far more meaningful competition will develop among *individual segments* of the various kinds of capitalism. Every aspect of a country's performance will be compared with the same aspects of other countries. If some features are found wanting, changes will often be made. Sometimes change will be in the direction of greater market control, sometimes in the direction of greater state capitalism.

For example, during the last several years the United States operated to a considerable extent under the belief that market forces could adequately regulate the financial industry. The subprime mortgage disaster followed. We will now, almost certainly, turn to greater government regulation of the financial markets. That will be a moderate shift toward *state* capitalism in an important sector of the economy. Another example. As the following chapter describes, three forces are driving government to a greater involvement in the U.S. health care system. Again, that will be a shift toward *state* capitalism. It will *not* be a shift toward socialism. Socialism would require government ownership of hospitals, clinics, and laboratories. It would also require all health care providers to be employees of the government.

China provides an example of a much-needed shift in the opposite direction. As described in the previous chapter, China has a grossly inefficient agriculture system. It could achieve greater total output with perhaps 10-to-20 percent of its current farm-labor force by turning to private ownership of farmland, including a free market for that land. When it comes, that will be a major shift to market management away from state capitalism.

In the competition between capitalism and state capitalism there will be many winners and losers in different economic sectors. Change will be made in both directions. Governments will learn from one another as they try to solve their problems. What a dynamic and productive learning environment the coming decades will provide as competition develops among various sectors of the world's economies, each with a different proportion of market and state control.

The ability of the United States to compete with countries that are more state-capitalist will depend as much on how we manage our economy as on how other countries manage theirs. If we keep borders open to trade and investment, reduce monopolies in business and labor, educate, train, and retrain our citizens, continually work toward efficient government, and maintain sufficient aggregate demand to keep our workers employed, we will be able to compete with any country, state capitalist or market capitalist.

The Trade Deficit

A great many people are afraid that the United States will be unable to compete in the world economy, especially with developing countries using cheap labor and our modern technology. Probably the most important single factor behind that fear is our large trade deficit with the rest of the world. We are reminded of that deficit daily when we shop. We have been buying a growing part of our needs from abroad. Many people are afraid of losing their jobs to foreign workers.

The United States is currently buying about $600 billion more goods and services from abroad each year than it is selling abroad. We are paying for those excessive imports by borrowing from abroad and by selling off some American assets such as stocks, real estate, and whole companies. Foreigners currently own about $2.5 trillion more of American assets and debt than Americans own of foreign assets ($2.5 trillion is equal to about one-fifth of our GDP). Our trade imbalance has been growing annually. How can it be corrected?

International trade imbalances of this sort are usually corrected *automatically* by market forces operating on currency exchange rates. The large amount of dollars flooding onto the foreign exchange markets to buy foreign goods should force the dollar down against foreign currencies, making foreign goods more expensive to Americans and American goods less expensive to foreigners. Imports should decline and exports should rise, closing the trade gap. Why has it not yet happened? There are two reasons. First, because of the *successes* of the American economy. America has been seen as a safe place to invest. Its financial markets are massive, so large sums can be moved in and out of the country quickly. Strong growth has led to relatively high interest rates, attracting bond buyers. All these factors have bid up the price of the dollar in relation to other currencies, encouraging imports and discouraging exports.

Second, in the last few years, another more problematic force has prevented the dollar from declining enough to close the huge trade deficit. *China, Japan, and some other countries have not let it decline.* They have supported the price of the dollar by buying it on the foreign exchange market. They have wanted to keep and expand their international markets and protect their home markets. By keeping their currencies low against the dollar they have demonstrated that acquiring and retaining export markets is a higher priority than buying necessary goods cheaply, which they could do if they let their own currencies rise. Put another way, they are hogging markets that would otherwise be taken by firms in other countries, both advanced and developing, and they are doing it at the cost of paying excessive prices for the things they import and going without some things they desperately need. Other developing countries should be complaining loudly that China is stealing their markets by manipulating its currency's exchange rate.

The United States *by itself* can do little to *quickly* reduce its trade deficit without seriously harming itself and others. But happily, other governments will reduce *our* trade deficit *as they learn to adopt policies that will be beneficial to their own countries.* Which countries will help close the American trade gap as they move to improve their own economies?

China's Choice

China for several years has been pegging its currency, the yuan, at an unrealistically low level against the dollar, boosting exports and restraining imports. Consequently, it has built up an enormous trade surplus with the United States. The dollars received from the excessive exports have been used to buy United States Treasury securities. China now owns about $800 billion of the U.S. debt.

At the same time that China (still a poor country) has been producing and exporting huge quantities of goods to the United States (a rich country), *it has been going without a lot of things it desperately needs.* Chinese cities are among the most polluted in the world. China needs better infrastructure of many kinds. It desperately needs better health care and old age support. China has chosen to build up productive resources for *export* goods rather than build up productive resources for *domestic uses* so badly needed. That policy is beginning to change under pressure of rising discontent of the Chinese populace.

China will begin satisfying domestic needs by more government spending, which will, in turn, spur spending by the Chinese people. To keep the economy from overheating, they will let the yuan rise. The prices of imports will decline and total imports will rise. Exports will grow more slowly because the higher yuan will make them more expensive. Then China can divert the workers coming off its inefficient farms and from state-owned plants that are being closed into building up industries for domestic production. They will produce badly needed goods for local use instead of goods for export. It's a win-win situation for China. Production for domestic consumption will be far better for China than maintaining a cheap yuan, increasing exports and building up holdings of American securities. Increasing China's imports without increasing exports will help reduce America's trade deficit. China will buy more goods from the United States and from other countries that will buy more goods from the United States.

In summary, China will simply be channeling its growing productive resources more toward production for internal consumption and less to production for export. Also, the increased value of the yuan on the foreign exchange market will allow China to buy oil and other imports at a lower price and thus help existing structural competition to hold down prices, making rapid growth possible.

Oil Exporters' Investments

In the past few years, the rising price of oil has thrown another complication into the international trade mechanism. The trade surpluses of oil-exporting countries have grown by hundreds of billions of dollars. The U.S. trade deficit has been impacted in two ways. The deficit has widened due to the higher cost of imported oil. But also important, the huge amounts of cash received by oil exporters have so far been partly saved. A substantial part of the money received by the oil exporters from *all* oil importers (not just from the United States) has been converted to dollars and invested partly in United States Treasury securities (often through the London financial markets). The increased demand for dollars to buy U.S. securities has raised the dollar's price on the foreign exchange market, making imports into the United States cheaper and United States exports more expensive to foreigners. Consequently our trade deficit has widened.

Oil exporters have started to spend more of those petrodollars. Although oil prices have declined from recent extremes, the rapid growth of the new capitalist world will likely prevent prices dropping to the average price in the twenties that prevailed for many years. Recession-induced price weaknesses will not likely last long. Furthermore, oil-exporting countries have begun to invest their oil revenues in projects throughout the region and around the world. Many of those dollars will be used to buy American goods, reducing our trade deficit. That investment by oil exporting countries will be much better for the oil exporters and the world than buying United States Treasury securities.

Japan's Learning Challenge

Japan is an important example of a country that has suffered from a stagnant economy *resulting from inadequate demand* that did *not* stem from policies needed to curb continuing inflation. It was caused initially by the bursting of the twin bubbles in stocks and real estate in 1989. The wealth effect of declining stock and real estate values reduced consumer demand. Unable to successfully get its economy moving adequately by monetary policy, Japan kept the yen artificially low by intervention in the foreign exchange market. This intervention boosted Japan's exports and restrained imports. Japan was attempting to offset its failure to increase domestic demand by increasing foreign demand. That action was a significant cause of the U.S. trade deficit and the decline of the U.S. automobile industry. Japan now shows evidence of relying more on internal consumption rather than exports to achieve faster growth.

Reducing the Trade Deficit: Not Quick or Painless

The U.S. trade deficit will be reduced. The worry of many people that the Chinese and workers in other countries will take over more and more of our markets, creating widespread unemployment, is misplaced. Imports from China and elsewhere have caused the shifting of jobs but have not increased overall unemployment. The coming reduction in the trade deficit will be neither quick nor painless. A decline of the dollar against other currencies will likely be required to reduce the deficit. That makes imports more expensive, reducing the amount imported, and makes exports less expensive to foreign buyers, increasing the amount exported. The decline of the dollar against other currencies to close the trade deficit *may* be substantial, and that dollar decline could have unpleasant repercussions.

The increase in import prices will aggravate inflation, pushing the CPI closer to the ceiling that will bring Federal Reserve restraint, slowing the economy. Maintaining *very* full employment will be somewhat harder while the trade deficit is being reduced.

As indicated earlier, we are now importing about $600 billion a year more in goods and services than we are exporting. That amounts to about 5 percent of our GDP. To close the trade deficit we must reduce imports by 5 percent of GDP or increase exports by 5 percent of GDP, or a combination of the two. That adjustment compares to a normal annual growth rate of about 5 percent of

GDP. Such a large adjustment cannot be made quickly or easily. To make matters more difficult, that adjustment in imports and exports must be made in those industries that produce goods and services that are *traded on international markets*. Those industries are mainly manufacturing, agriculture, mining, and some services such as tourism. Internationally tradable goods and services amount to about a third of our GDP. That means that an adjustment of 5 percent of total GDP would amount to three times that percentage when concentrated in tradable goods industries—an adjustment of 15 percent. Decreasing imports or increasing exports (or a combination of the two) by 15 percent in those industries will likely take several years.

We should carry this analysis one step farther. Which groups of those tradable commodities will be impacted the most? Will our imports of low-skill, high-labor-content goods such as clothing, shoes, and toys decline? Probably not. As Chinese wages rise rapidly and the Chinese yuan rises against the dollar, imports will shift to products made in India, Bangladesh, Vietnam, Indonesia, or perhaps some African or Caribbean countries where low wages and low exchange rates may persist. So it will be many years before imports of low-skill, high-labor-content goods decline very far. Therefore that adjustment amounting to about 15 percent in tradable goods will be concentrated even more in higher-end goods and services. That cannot happen quickly. To close the trade deficit, a rapid increase in the production of high-end goods in the United States must be realized. Demand for these high-end goods from other countries will increase as capitalism spreads throughout the world.

Elsewhere in this book I have noted that worldwide competition impinges most severely at this time on the unskilled worker rather than the skilled. That competitive differential will one day be lifted as capitalism spreads around the world, but it won't be complete for many years. So, as the following chapter argues, we had better take advantage of the several ways available to improve our education system and improve our workers' skills.

What effect will closing the trade deficit have on our standard of living? For years we have been consuming more goods and services than we have produced, importing the difference. As we reduce the trade deficit our growth in consumption must slow. If the trade deficit is closed in 10 years, our growth in consumption of goods and services will slow by 0.5 of a percentage point a year as a result of that closing. That will be noticeable but not disastrous.

The Twin Deficits

The federal budget deficit and the U.S. trade deficit are sometimes referred to as the twin deficits, implying that the trade deficit could be reduced by reducing the budget deficit. The federal budget is far too cumbersome to be used for reducing the trade deficit quickly, but it can help to reduce the deficit gradually over time.

The most common economic environment to be expected in the future will be periods of expanding business activity with inflation under reasonable control, more so than recession or excessive inflation. At such time, unilateral action taken to gradually reduce any existing federal budget deficit will help to reduce the trade deficit. A federal budget deficit means the government is pouring more money into the spending-income stream than it is taking out. That means it is stimulating the economy. The larger the deficit the greater the stimulation, and the greater the pressure for the Federal Reserve to keep interest rates high to prevent the economy from overheating. High interest rates attract investment from abroad. When foreigners buy dollars to buy American securities, they drive up the price of the dollar on the foreign exchange market. Imports become cheaper to Americans and exports become more expensive to foreigners. The tendency is for the trade deficit to widen. In summary, large budget deficits *tend* to produce large trade deficits. But the federal budget is cumbersome, slow to change. It cannot be used to effect *quick* changes in the trade deficit.

The federal government should *always* be working toward a balanced budget, but how should we define a "balanced budget"? As stated in Chapter 5, a budget should be considered balanced *if existing tax rates will produce revenue that will match expenditures at a full-employment level of business activity*. For example, if the country drops into recession, tax receipts will automatically decline at the lower level of business activity. The budget deficit will widen.

That should *not* call for increased tax rates. Economic recovery will increase tax revenues to reduce the deficit.

In summary, tax and expenditures policies should be long term in nature. Monetary policy and stimulative distributions to consumers (as described in Chapter 5) should be used to make necessary short-term adjustments to the level of business activity and to inflation. Changes in the trade deficit must remain an incidental by-product in the effort to maintain full employment, control inflation, and balance the federal budget.

Reducing the Trade Deficit by Increasing Trade Barriers

Tariffs, import quotas, and other devices to limit international competition are frequently proposed to reduce the trade deficit and to protect American jobs. They rarely work, either on a short-term or long-term basis. They provoke retaliation and have the potential of seriously damaging the American as well as the world economy. They should be nonstarters. Policies to maintain *very* full employment as described in Chapters 4 and 5 help to reduce the pressure for adopting trade barriers.

Reducing the Trade Deficit by Increasing Structural Competition

As pointed out in numerous places in this book, the intensification of structural competition must *always* be of great concern. Policies to improve the intensity of competition built into the structure of the economy are *all* of a long-term nature. They cannot be changed quickly to meet a short-term crisis. But over time, improving the intensity of structural competition, with its more effective inflation control, allows the Federal Reserve to keep interest rates lower than otherwise. Demand for American securities by foreign buyers is kept low, reducing upward pressure on the dollar. Imports are restrained, and exports are maintained. Upward pressure on the trade deficit is reduced.

We can add the ability to help correct the trade deficit to all the other splendid virtues of intense structural competition.

Flexible Foreign Exchange Rates

Flexible foreign exchange rates are necessary to allow each country to adjust *gradually* to changes in other countries. These changes include different growth rates, different inflation rates, and special events like little wars that impact each country in a different way. More than a century ago when capitalism was in its early childhood, governments put the world into an economic straitjacket called the gold standard. All countries were expected to keep the value of their currencies constant in relation to a fixed weight of gold. The United States, for example, was expected to always be ready to buy or sell gold at $20.67 an ounce. Since the value of each currency was fixed in relation to an ounce of gold, the value of each currency was fixed in relation to the value of every other currency. The level of economic activity and prices in each country had to adjust to the fixed gold-currency relationship.

The gold standard has been called a "fair weather" standard. When a crisis occurred governments simply suspended gold payments and abandoned the standard. Indeed, the rigidity of the gold standard, in actual practice, prevented *gradual* adjustments to differential changes among countries and actually *led* to crises. Then, when crises developed, foolish policies were often adopted such as the U.S. government's actions early in the Great Depression. We tightened money to protect the value of the dollar on the foreign exchange market. We increased taxes and choked off international trade. We turned a middle-sized business decline into the Great Depression.

The gold standard died in World War I. It has been resuscitated briefly a couple of times since then. Also, individual countries have for short periods attempted to fix the price of their currencies in relation to some other currency. These attempts to fix the value of currencies have often ended badly. They have often precipitated financial panics and recessions. All in all, the trend has been away from the rigid exchange rates of the gold standard toward flexible exchange rates. As capitalism has moved out of its childhood, we have learned much about the importance of flexible exchange rates to make the gradual adjustments necessary to sustain international trade. They will gradually correct our current trade imbalance.

Competition in Science and Technology

We frequently read of the hundreds of thousands of engineers being turned out annually by India and China and of American companies opening research facilities in those countries. Are these developments ominous indicators that the Asians will take over high-end science and technology as they have taken over much of low-end manufacturing? Things are not as ominous as they seem. A very large part of those Asian engineers are civil engineers needed for the massive construction projects under way in those countries. And a large proportion of engineers are graduating from second-rate schools. But that is changing. Some schools are already of excellent quality and others are improving. Competition at the high end of the worldwide labor force will gradually increase. Considering the sheer size of the Asian population, there is little doubt that by the end of the capitalist twenty-first century more high-quality scientists and engineers will be living in Asia than in America. But the worldwide demand for high-end goods and services will grow rapidly. As the dollar declines in value on the foreign exchange market and as wages and salaries of scientists and engineers rise in other countries, high-end jobs will still be readily available in this country for those who are prepared for them.

Even if Asia, with its huge population, eventually makes more discoveries and inventions than America, will that matter? We must distinguish between *making* new scientific discoveries and technological inventions on one hand and the *use* of those discoveries and developments on the other hand. Every region would like to make its share of discoveries and inventions. They add to both profit and prestige. But *making* the discoveries and inventions is not absolutely essential for each country. A discovery or invention made in one country spreads around the world carrying its benefits to other countries. The speed of that transfer will accelerate. Each nation's companies are rapidly expanding into other countries, so an invention made by a company in one country is quickly adopted by branches of that company in other countries. Also, companies sell their products throughout the world, and they license their inventions to companies in other countries. Technology transfer is *dependent mainly on the ability and willingness of countries to receive it.* In the twenty-second century we may not be making as many discoveries and inventions as the vast Asian population, but we will benefit from their discoveries as they will benefit from ours.

What conditions are essential for making and adopting new discoveries and inventions? Chapter 3 described three conditions that are important for problem solving—a *large number of capable participants* with *opportunities* to innovate, and *driven by competition* to do so. Those conditions are necessary for both making and adopting discoveries and inventions. Governments that want to modernize must support all three conditions.

A first-class educational system is, of course, necessary to produce large numbers of highly capable participants for the innovation process. At the important high end of our educational system, U.S. universities have excelled in the sciences and professions. But new universities in Asia will eventually become equally proficient as they copy America's winners and tie into the international discovery network of private firms, universities, private research organizations, and governments. Asia will eventually surpass America in the *quantity* of innovators but will not necessarily excel in the *capability* of those innovators. As new ideas flow throughout the international interconnected world, the other two requirements for adopting technological development will grow in importance— *opportunity* to innovate and *competitive pressure* to do so.

Governments that close their borders to trade and investment reduce both opportunity to innovate and competitive pressure to do so. Governments that maintain a *monopoly culture*, protecting "champion" industries, will also reduce opportunities and competitive pressure to innovate. A well-developed financial system is necessary to provide opportunities for qualified innovators, thus increasing competition. Altogether, the factors that make for a well-functioning capitalist market provide the requirements for rapid innovation. The United States should prevail.

Chapter 8

SOCIAL SERVICES IN THE
CAPITALIST CENTURY

An efficient, well-designed social services system is a clear necessity in a capitalist economy. Social services have saved capitalism. They have mitigated the difficulties caused by capitalism's income inequality and therefore prevented the tearing apart of the social fabric that Greenspan fears will yet proceed from that inequality if it is not corrected. Those fears were described in Chapter 1. Income inequality is inevitable under capitalism. Human beings have widely divergent capabilities due to differing genetic and nurturing heritages. In a capitalist economy we sell those widely divergent capabilities in the market. Income inequality is inevitable. Even though social services have saved capitalism, they have sometimes damaged capitalism when badly designed. Since social services absorb such a large part of a country's output, the efficiency of social services will go a long way toward determining the efficiency of the entire economy. What should the United States do to improve the efficiency of social services?

The Heart of the Inequality Problem

People come into this world with a genetic heritage that to some unknown extent but at least partially, perhaps substantially, determines their personalities, talents, intelligence, appearance, health, and energy. These qualities are molded through a nurturing process throughout childhood and adolescence. The quality of that nurturing process varies from individual to individual just as the genetic heritage varies from one person to another. Each person then is thrown into a highly *competitive environment*, socially and economically. That environment is a gigantic sorting machine. It puts individuals into little metaphorical boxes whose dimensions and nature of restraints are determined by genetic and nurturing heritage. People often cannot understand the nature of those restraints. They spend their lives contending with the demons and enjoying the talents embedded in their genetic and nurturing heritage. Some people have more demons than talents.

Now add other complications to the mix. People who are richly endowed by genetic heritage and quality of nurturing *tend* to marry people also richly endowed, usually producing children who are richly endowed. Richly endowed people are generally successful financially, so they can add a dollop of material wealth to the genetic and nurturing endowments they give to their children. They can also provide valuable social, business, and professional connections. People who are poorly endowed *tend* to marry people also poorly endowed, usually producing children who are poorly endowed. No one can predict with precision which demons and talents the genetic lottery will cast up in a particular child, but those demons and talents that existed most often in previous generations will *tend* to prevail.

Genetic and nurturing heritage is the most important factor in determining social and economic performance. A simple intelligence test given young people is the best *single* predictor of economic performance. Students with IQ scores between 70 and 85 are often classified as slow learners. They lack the intelligence to keep up with the class but are not slow enough to qualify as handicapped or needing special education. These individuals make up 10 to 15 percent of the population, larger than the group of children with learning disabilities, mental retardation, and autism combined. Slow learners account for a disproportionate number of school dropouts, unwed teen mothers, illicit drug users, functionally illiterate persons, incarcerated persons, unemployed, underemployed, violent offenders, alcohol abusers, school failures, and gang and hate group members. In other words, slow learners can *disproportionately* account for nearly every major problem within education and society.[9]

An individual cannot be blamed for a defective genetic heritage nor for defective early nurturing. Does government have any special responsibility toward those who perform badly in the competitive struggle *because of their defective heritage*? That is a question that governments will face repeatedly as affluence grows in the coming capitalist century and as demands for social services increase. Designing social service policies would be far easier if all people had the same talents and handicaps. But they don't. The differences lie at the heart of many social service problems.

You may think governments should give special support to the poorly endowed to help preserve social tranquility. Or your values may be such that you think governments should aid the poorly endowed simply out of humanitarian considerations. Whatever your reasons, if you feel governments should help ease the path of the less-endowed, you must make a judgment as to *what* governments should do to make sure they do more good than harm.

Problems exist whenever we provide social services such as education, welfare, old age pensions, and health care to everyone, but the really serious problems arise in providing social services to the poorly endowed. That's when special attention and wisdom are required.

Three Classes of Social Services

We will consider just three categories of government-provided social services:

Basic services include the maintenance of full employment and the provision of quality education. Unless jobs can be obtained with reasonable ease and unless education is available to prepare people for those jobs, the economy will function poorly and other social services will be overburdened. A job is the ticket to the personal independence and responsibility that capitalism requires.

Insurance is provided by most advanced countries against the costs of illness, disability, and old age.

"Nanny" state services and controls include welfare and the prison system. A capitalist democracy can perform well only when the great majority of people take responsibility for their own welfare and for behavior that stays within the rules of society. When people cannot (or will not) take personal responsibility, the state steps in to take charge as a "nanny" state. Obviously, if many people require state support, direction, and control, the burden will be great and the performance of the country will be poor.

We consider only two categories of people who inhabit the nanny state—those in prison and those on *means-tested* welfare. Those in prison are there because some court has decreed that, at least for a time, they are not capable of taking, or willing to take, responsibility for their own behavior. Those on means-tested welfare are there because they have proven to some government functionary that they have insufficient assets and income to care for themselves. They have failed to take responsibility for their economic welfare. The nanny state is the social service of last resort. It follows when all else fails. It will be described toward the end of this chapter, but first we must examine some policies that will help keep people out of the clutches of the nanny state.

Maintaining Very Full Employment

Maintaining full employment is the basic social service. Without full employment, other social services are overburdened, and the economy performs badly. Only government (including the central bank) can maintain full employment by the management of aggregate demand and structural competition. Capitalism is a partnership between the market and the state. It failed abominably during the Great Depression and performed poorly even up to the period of awakening, when it slipped out of its childhood into a spirited adolescence. It has yet to mature.

Maintaining full employment, *very* full employment, is absolutely essential to provide both *opportunities* and *incentives*, especially for the less-endowed. Help wanted signs popping up on the street provide a glimmer of opportunity that can encourage initiative. High unemployment rates bear most heavily on the unskilled. Besides reducing their employment opportunities more than those of the richly endowed, high unemployment puts greater downward pressure on the *wages* of the unskilled.

U.S. capitalism has made great progress toward full employment. In the inflationary 1970s, unemployment *averaged* about 7 percent. In the recession required to break that inflation, unemployment rose to almost 11 percent. In the decade prior to 2008 which included a recession, unemployment averaged only about 5 percent. It only once reached 6 percent. However, as described in Chapter 5, failure to maintain the quality of credit resulted in the subprime mortgage crisis beginning in 2008 that has produced another serious recession. If we fail to take bold stimulating action, unemployment could match the 11 percent reached in 1982.

Most of the learning episodes that have made the improvement possible have been described elsewhere in this book.

• The inflationary 1970s taught us to attack inflation early before expectations of accelerating inflation become well established. We have not had high unemployment caused by inflation since the inflationary 1970s and aftermath.

• We learned how to improve the intensity of structural competition by opening borders to greater foreign competition. That foreign competition has become one of the most powerful job *creators* we have, because it reduces the necessity for below-capacity competition with its high unemployment to curb inflation. Improving structural competition further as described in Chapter 4 can enhance our quest for *very* full employment.

• We learned to use fiscal stimulus to aid monetary stimulus to keep recessions short. Much more should be done to make this a *flexible* fiscal stimulus as described in Chapter 5.

• We learned in the early 1990s to use "tough love" to require welfare recipients to get jobs after a period of time on welfare. This is but the beginning of a program to require welfare recipients to prepare for a job, look for a job, take a job, and *hold* a job whenever it is reasonably possible.

• We learned to improve work incentives for lower income workers with the Earned Income Tax Credit (EITC). The EITC is a cash supplement paid by the federal government to low-income wage earners. It is claimed when the worker files his income tax return. The EITC was designed to supplement low-wage rates to *increase incentives* to work and to *reduce hardship* for low-income workers. Numerous studies have shown that the EITC increases labor force participation among low-skilled workers. Studies have also specifically linked the growth in the EITC to the growth in the number of single mothers moving from welfare to work. For example, it is estimated that between 1993 and 2000, employment participation among single mothers rose from 58 to almost 74 percent, leading to a decline in the poverty rate among their children from 46 to 33 percent.

Under the 2008 tax code, a family of four with earned income up to about $12,000 and with no other income would receive a payment amounting to 40 percent of their wage earnings. That helps to reduce the hardships of low-wage earners while improving incentives to work. (For workers with earned income above $12,000, the payment as a percentage of income declines rapidly with higher incomes. The payment is also reduced if the worker has income other than earned income.)

Serious problems of fraud and overpayment have been experienced. Some of them have been corrected, but it is doubtful that they will ever be eliminated. Nevertheless, the EITC appears to be a workable device to increase the income and the incentives to work for the less-endowed. The EITC fits the major requirements that should guide policies to aid the poorly endowed. It increases incentives and obligates the recipient to work. It is a valuable aid to achieving *very* full employment.

Unfortunately we have also had a couple of learning failures. In the most critical failure we did *not* learn to preserve by regulation a high quality of credit in the financial system as described in Chapter 5. Because of that failure we are now (early 2009) in a serious recession. Our painful experience with the subprime mortgage and related credit problems will certainly improve our management of the quality of credit and the overall exposure to debt of our banking system. It will turn out to be an important learning episode.

Immigration control has also been a failure. Uncontrolled immigration has substantially lowered wages for unskilled workers in some areas and some jobs. This low pay has made many jobs both in cities and on farms unattractive to many Americans and added to the unemployment rate for the unskilled.

Immigration, like merchandise imports, tends to hold down the inflation rate and therefore reduces the need for below-capacity competition with its increased overall unemployment. However, *uncontrolled, illegal* immigration bears especially heavily on the poorly endowed in areas where immigrants congregate, having a serious negative effect on the wages and employment of low-income, low-skill workers. Our borders should be more tightly controlled. Immigration is valuable in holding down inflation, but it should be controlled so that its effects are less concentrated on the unskilled.

One part of immigration ought to be substantially *expanded*. The federal government's H-1B visas program enables companies to get special temporary visas (which often turn into permanent green cards) for potential employees with special skills. But they are limited by *quota*, first come, first served. For the last few years, that quota has been quickly exhausted because the demand has been so great. The program should be sharply expanded. It would help control inflation without impinging too heavily on any one group. Diversified immigration would allow quicker cultural absorption.

To repeat, maintaining full employment is the most basic of all social services. Properly managed, full employment will help keep people out of the clutches of the nanny state with its prisons and means-tested welfare rolls.

A Promising Experiment in Education

Elementary and secondary education in the United States has performed poorly compared to education in many other advanced countries. Any deficiency in school performance is intolerable in light of the growing complexity of our society and increased world-wide competition. Also, improving education is one of the best ways of keeping people out of the clutches of the nanny state.

Fortunately, a little over a decade ago, several cities and states began a remarkable experiment that may make a substantial improvement. *Parental choice, competition among schools to attract students, and greater freedom to innovate* were introduced in a new education program. Charter schools, school vouchers, and corporate tax credits for scholarships were the vehicles for this improvement. In spite of unrelenting opposition, especially by teachers unions, the experiment has been successful. Growth has been substantial. We may be near the tipping point where the magnitude of the problem of education deficiency and the success of past experience with the new programs will produce a dramatic change in education.

Chapter 3 described the best conditions for problem solving: the existence of many qualified participants with the opportunity to innovate and under competitive pressure to do so. These new school systems have the necessary qualifications.

Charter Schools

Charter schools are special schools largely financed by government but managed outside the regular school system and, in several states, free from many of the regulations that govern the regular schools. Since they began in Minnesota in 1992, growth has been substantial. Nearly 4,000 schools serve more than a million students, about 2 percent of the elementary and secondary school population in the United States. These schools do not attract students by extensive advertising campaigns. They attract students by "word of mouth" recommendations. They must please parents by the quality of education. They have done so.

The quality of charter school education compared with that of public schools was examined by Harvard economist Caroline Hoxby.[10] Her study is one of the most important and comprehensive studies on charter schools done to date. She sampled schools that enroll 99 percent of all charter elementary school students. Standardized test scores for students in these schools were compared to test scores *in public schools that students would likely have attended if there were no charter schools*. By using this comparison method, Hoxby was able to compare "apples to apples" and answer the question "What kind of education would charter school students receive if there were no charter schools?"

Hoxby's data, based on matching, indicate that charter school students are 5.2 percent more likely to be proficient in reading and 3.2 percent more likely to be proficient in math on their state exams compared to students in matched public schools. The results are even more significant for disadvantaged students. The data suggest that in predominately Hispanic areas, the proficiency advantage of charter schools is 7.6 percent in reading and 4.1 percent in math. For charter schools in high poverty areas, the proficiency advantage in reading is 6.5 percent.

The Hoxby data do *not* show that charter schools, in their short life span, have discovered dramatically better ways to educate elementary students. The data show that somewhat more charter school students become proficient in reading and math, but they do not show *how much* more. Remarkably, the better performance of charter schools is achieved with *substantially less government funding* per enrolled student than public schools receive. The competition to public schools provided by charter schools appears to be bringing some improvement to public schools. As the charter school movement matures perhaps this competition will bring the greatest benefit to public education.

Charter schools are disproportionately based in inner cities, serving disadvantaged students, many of whom are poorly endowed, slow learners. That is precisely the place where our most serious education problems lie. Expansion of charter schools may be part of the solution. Two other facts are of paramount importance. Charter schools under the most restrictive regulation by the state perform worst. Schools that are better financed by government perform best.

School Vouchers

Under the *voucher system*, the city or state provides vouchers to parents authorizing the student to attend the school of choice among those private schools that accept vouchers. A major, practical difference between charter schools and the voucher system is that vouchers can be used at religious schools. Also, private schools that accept vouchers are far less subject to regulation than charter schools.

Vouchers have been adopted in only a few jurisdictions. However, where they have been adopted they have shown impressive growth. Milwaukee, Wisconsin, the voucher pioneer, provides vouchers to nearly 20 percent of the public school population. The city pays only half to two thirds as much for educating a voucher student as a regular public school student. If all voucher students were to return to public schools, Milwaukee public school costs would rise more than $70 million a year. In addition, they would have to build many new school buildings. The quality of teaching, on average, in voucher schools is at least as good as in the average public school. Parents of those students who attend voucher schools certainly think so. A large proportion of Milwaukee's voucher students attend religious schools.

There are more than 20,000 religious elementary and secondary schools in the United States, teaching nearly 10 percent of the nation's students. There is some evidence that religious schools are somewhat better at keeping students in school until graduation, and many of these students go on to college. We are desperately in need of ways to inspire students to stay in school. Should not our religious schools be regarded as a valuable resource to achieve that end? Many parents would love to gain the support of a religious school to help keep their children out of trouble if only they could afford it.

Corporate tax credits for scholarships achieve basically the same results as the voucher system. Scholarships can be used at any qualified private school that will accept them, including religious schools. They are designed especially to aid underprivileged children. They are a new development.

No Child Left Behind

The No Child Left Behind Act addresses one of the most important problems in American education. How can we improve the learning performance of the poorly endowed, slow learners? It is a daunting task. We have to find a way to bring out the best in millions of poorly endowed children (often from low-income families), motivating them to study hard when studying is difficult, and when it will likely help them gain at best only a modest income. Many of the children already have had a few years of failure with the accompanying loss of confidence. They have few personal role models to induce them to study.

The title of the act, "No Child Left Behind," sets it up for failure. Many children will be left behind. But the act does a great service in focusing attention on the slow learner. We should do our best to test the limits of what we can do to help the slow learner by one-on-one tutoring, special classes, *tying school more closely to jobs*, and other techniques yet to be discovered by educators given the freedom to innovate and under competitive pressure to do so. We must do more to keep slow learners out of the clutches of the nanny state. So far, the promise of the Act that a parent will have the option of transferring a child from a failing school has not been fully implemented. There are not enough places in good schools to absorb all the students now in failing schools. Perhaps the students will have to be placed in charter or voucher schools.

Minorities in cities, where our most serious school problems exist, can take a dramatic step toward improved schools by well-organized demands that parents be given the right to choose their children's schools as an *important part of their civil rights*. That choice must include the right to attend charter and/or voucher schools. Few initiatives would do more for the well-being of inner city residents than this extension of civil rights.

Then there are the underachievers. These are the students who are sufficiently endowed intellectually to perform well in school but are failing to learn because of poor teaching in poor schools. They are grist for the mills of those who want so badly to improve the quality of teaching in our schools.

Social Security

The governments of all advanced countries protect their citizens against various risks, the two most common being the problems of old age and the costs of ill health. The problem of financing Social Security has been getting a lot of attention in the United States, but actually it will be one of the easiest of our social service problems to solve.

Workable corrections are well known. All that is needed is a compromise among policy makers regarding which of the corrective policies should be emphasized. That compromise will be forthcoming as the lack of funding to meet currently promised benefits becomes imminent. Probable solutions will be described in Chapter 9 in connection with the problems of the aging population.

Health Care

The condition of the U.S. health care system is so onerous that major efforts to change it will be forthcoming in the next several years. Three powerful forces will be driving those changes:

1. Over 47 million people are without health insurance. The devastation to many of them caused by unaffordable health care is being reported regularly. That publicity is bringing a groundswell of opinion that greater health insurance coverage is needed. Employer-provided health care is failing in many small

125

companies, swelling the ranks of the uninsured. Many people are afraid they will lose their insurance.

2. Health care in the United States currently costs over $2 trillion a year. That is about 16 percent of our total output of goods and services. It is up from about 9 percent in 1980 and is expected to rise to about 20 percent by 2015. The cost of health care in the United States relative to GDP is about twice that of most advanced countries. Medicaid and SCHIP, the two programs for the indigent, are absorbing a growing share of state budgets, seriously crowding out other critical services. Health care costs are also taking a growing percentage of total workers' compensation in the private sector, thereby slowing the growth of wages. That slow growth of wages has not gone unnoticed. The trend of rising health care costs is too steep to be tolerated for long.

3. Almost everyone who has studied the present health care system agrees that it is beset by flagrant inefficiencies and waste. Even the *quality* of care for the *average patient* is coming into question. A growing array of books and articles describes these defects. People in other advanced countries, on average, live longer than Americans even though their countries spend far less per person on health care than we do. That is some evidence of the inefficiencies of our system.

Four groups should be considered when examining these three driving forces: Three of them—the uninsured, those protected by Medicaid, and those insured by Medicare—each contain approximately 15 percent of the U.S. population. People with employer-provided insurance and some individually-insured individuals make up the balance. These percentages are rough approximations, but listing three of them at 15 percent makes them easier to remember.

When evaluating possible health care proposals for each of these groups, we must keep three goals in mind: access, maintenance of quality, and cost control. Cost and quality must be considered together. Efforts to restrain costs must be appraised in relation to the impact on quality. Efforts to improve quality must be appraised in relation to the effect on costs.

The U.S. health care system is so complex, and so many people have personal and financial stakes in various parts of the system, that an overarching, disruptive reorganization of the system as tried by the Clinton administration is not likely to be attempted. But incremental steps will likely be taken that will lead to a far different health care system over the next several years. A description of some of those likely changes follows, along with a few suggestions for changes I believe *should* be made.

Step 1. Providing Health Insurance Access for the Uninsured

The federal government will subsidize health insurance for those who cannot afford it. The mechanics will be difficult, and the program will be expensive, but subsidized insurance will come, possibly enacted before the end of 2009. That will still leave many people uninsured. Many of these people can afford insurance but choose not to buy it. They often show up at hospital emergency rooms when sick. Service cannot be denied. The hospital bills are often unpaid, and the cost to the hospital increases the prices regular patients must pay.

Consequently, mandates will likely be imposed to guarantee insurance coverage. Those mandates *may* require all large businesses to provide insurance to their employees. However, this will not have great effect since most companies with over 200 employees already provide health insurance. Imposing mandates on small companies will be far more difficult, but will likely be tried. It will reduce the amount of subsidies to be paid by the government. Mandates requiring *individuals* to purchase health insurance will be adopted eventually, if not immediately. They will be necessary to keep emergency room costs down and to make possible the requirement that insurance companies accept all applicants *regardless of preexisting conditions*. Otherwise the insurance system would become burdened with a disproportionate percentage of less-healthy patients. With subsidies and mandates, near universal coverage will be achieved. By embarking on a system of universal health insurance, we will set in motion a chain of events that will significantly change our health care system. What will those changes be?

Step 2. A National Insurance Exchange

Several problems will be faced in providing insurance for 47 million people currently uninsured. Some of those problems will likely be met by the establishment of a National Insurance Exchange. This is a market on which any individual, regardless of preexisting health conditions, will be able to buy health insurance at *low group rates*. Since everyone will eventually be required to buy insurance, the program will avoid the problem of attracting only the less-healthy part of the population. Use of the National Health Exchange will not be limited to individuals. Small companies often have difficulty buying insurance for their employees at low group rates. They will have access to the exchange and will want to use it to keep insurance costs low.

A no-frills policy with small copayments should be the standard policy offered by all insurance companies. Small copayments may be necessary to avoid frivolous demands on health care resources. It should be a good policy with needed coverage, but not include some procedures such as infertility treatments. This basic policy should be designed by government but should not be financed or administered by government. That is, it should not be government insurance. A government insurance plan has enormous implications to be described in Step 9.

The basic no-frills policy should be subsidized for people with low incomes. Government cannot afford to subsidize more expensive, elaborate insurance. A *standardized*, basic, age-adjusted insurance policy is necessary to maintain strong competition among insurance companies to keep premiums low, and to avoid excessive insurance company profits. Many markets have demonstrated that a standardized, "undifferentiated" product becomes a "commodity" with strong competition and minimal profit margins to sellers. Yet, a variety of policies must be available to serve people with various needs.

Large companies with existing health insurance should be encouraged to offer two-part policies. The first part would be the basic, no-frills policy offered on the exchange. The second part would be a *basic-plus* policy that would match features offered by their existing insurance. These policies would also be offered through the insurance exchange. Insurance companies would, therefore, be competing to sell the standardized, basic policy that would potentially cover everyone except those insured by government through Medicare, Medicaid, and SCHIP. Insurance companies would also be competing to design and sell a variety of *basic-plus* policies to give people with varying needs a range of choice.

Step 3. Creating a National Health Board

With the drive toward universal health insurance coverage and the necessity of slowing the growth of health care costs, government is clearly taking a major step toward greater involvement in health care. That cannot be done effectively if the huge and complex health care system is designed and managed by Congress and the administration. *They are too much affected by day-to-day political forces. And they are far too slow in recognizing problems and making decisions.* We will likely have a National Health Board. Recommendations have been made that such a board be modeled after the Federal Reserve Board. It would have 5 to 10 members with staggered terms to preserve continuity. Members, appointed by the president, would have impeccable science and medical credentials and would be familiar with the practical problems of delivering health care.

The Board's major function would be one of design. It would design the rules governing subsidies and mandates to achieve universal coverage. It would design the structure of the National Insurance Exchange and the basic insurance policy to be offered on the Exchange. The design of medical networking infrastructure, best medical practices, wellness programs, a system for dealing with medical mistakes and malpractice insurance, and solutions to other problems would be on its agenda.

The Board would have the responsibility of recommending, and sometimes even determining, how our limited resources are to be used. How much should we devote to wellness programs? How much reserved to research and to which diseases? Eventually, far more difficult decisions may intrude on the Board's list of decision-making responsibilities. These decisions could require balancing the cost of using scarce resources against prolonging life itself. Should we provide several days' care in an expensive intensive care unit to keep alive a stroke victim who has little chance of surviving more than a few weeks, and that, in a near-helpless state? Should we devote extensive resources to try to keep alive low-weight, extremely premature babies that will likely be seriously handicapped for the few years they might live? Should we make huge monthly payments for medication that can keep a patient alive for a short time but cannot cure the ailment? Doctors and hospitals will be looking for support in making those decisions. In this difficult area the Board should only be able to make recommendations, not provide regulations. Yet, *cost* must be a consideration in the health care system.

Improving the design of our health care system should be an ongoing project for the Board. Our system must evolve continuously to meet new problems, to correct bad decisions, and to expand projects that work, such as community health centers for the poor. The Board would use the resources of the 27 National Institutes of Health to guide in the design of "best-practice" medical care. To provide guides for the most cost-effective medical practices, the Institutes would likely be greatly expanded. And, of course, the Board would have the support of an expert staff to help make decisions.

An extremely important function of the Board would be to encourage bottom-up experiments to improve our health care delivery system. Specifically, it should encourage various medical delivery centers to move away from our present fee-for-service system of paying for health care. These changes are emphasized in Step 10.

The Board, which would operate under authority granted by Congress, would have some regulatory authority. However, much of its ability to bring important improvements to health care would depend on its ability to *persuade* Congress and medical personnel in general to adopt its recommendations. And that would depend partly on its prestige. Prestige would depend initially on its members' credentials. Ultimately, that prestige would have to be earned by the wisdom of its decisions.

Step 4. Networking Infrastructure

Claims are often made that by computer networking we can

lower costs and improve cooperation among the doctors, hospitals, laboratories, and other facilities involved in treating a patient. A proposal has been made for a *national* computer-based network that will contain every patient's clinical history so that any doctor or hospital can get a patient's medical history quickly to aid in prescribing treatment. Funds have been appropriated for such a network. The design and testing of the system is the kind of project that should come under the guidance of a National Health Board. Exaggerated claims of the potential cost-saving will not likely be met.

Step 5. Best-Practice Determination

Startling reports are constantly surfacing about wide variations in medical practices among hospitals and doctors. Surprisingly, the most expensive practices are often not the most effective. The Board, with the aid of an expert staff, would have the responsibility of determining and recommending best practices. Data accumulated in computer networks might be mined to determine best practices and establish medical standards. Considerable cost saving might be achieved.

Step 6. Wellness Programs

These plans are always near the top of the list of ways to improve America's health and keep costs down. Not surprisingly, obesity and smoking are the main targets. Huge cost savings are possible if an effective program can be designed.

Step 7. Medical Mistakes and Malpractice Insurance

The Board must design changes to our unsatisfactory way of handling medical mistakes. At the present time, most patients who suffer from medical mistakes receive no compensation. A few receive large amounts from successful law suits. Doctors and hospitals have to pay outlandish premiums for malpractice insurance. Ezekiel J. Emanuel, writing in his book, *Health Care, Guaranteed*, suggests a major change. "Each of the twelve Regional

Health Boards will create a Center for Patient Safety and Dispute Resolution to receive and evaluate claims of injury by patients, compensate patients injured by medical error, and discipline or disqualify from practice those physicians found to be repeatedly injuring patients" (p. 83).[11] These new centers would largely replace the present court system for resolving malpractice claims. Such an approach should be considered. Besides being more equitable, it would substantially reduce health care costs by eliminating the necessity for doctors to practice defensive medicine.

Step 8. Shortage of Doctors and Nurses

The Board must have the responsibility for ensuring that an adequate number of doctors and nurses are being trained. A current shortage exists largely because a previous incorrect forecast underestimated the need. The shortage will not be quickly corrected because the elderly require more services than younger people, and the ranks of the elderly are growing.

Step 9. Controlling Health Care Costs

Most of the preceding eight steps for changing the health care system will likely materialize because they will be driven by the three forces described at the beginning of this section.

But now we come to the hard part. Unfortunately, the steps described so far may not slow the growth of health care costs sufficiently. Ultimately we may be forced to turn to some form of price control. How might such direct controls work out? Several approaches could be used. We will examine only two that have been widely recommended. First, controlling Medicare costs more rigorously and second, a government insurance plan to compete with private insurance plans.

Medicare already has a price-setting mechanism. It sets prices for thousands of medical procedures for each of several regions, but has not used that price-setting authority sufficiently to slow the growth of Medicare spending. Medicare costs *per enrollee* have increased 6 percent a year for the past 10 years. Total costs have grown more rapidly, amounting to $431 billion in 2007. At past growth rates, costs will double in less than 10 years. Medicare's growth is supported by lavish federal funding backed by a Congress that understands the power of the elderly-patient voting bloc. Some observers, including Mike Leavitt, former Secretary of the Department of Health and Human Services, claim that Medicare dominates much of health care in the United States. By example it drives the growth in costs, determines the choice of medical procedures and equipment, and influences many other aspects of health care. If this is true we must slow the growth of Medicare costs to slow the growth of all health care costs.

For several years, efforts have been made to cap total Medicare spending. Each time, Congress has refused. That refusal may continue as long as the current recession lasts and federal deficit spending is seen as helping to stimulate the economy. But in a year or two when recovery is well on its way, federal deficits will receive great attention. Fear of inflation will be pervasive. It will be accompanied by the expectation that the Federal Reserve will stand ready to raise interest rates to counter inflation, raising fears of another recession. Under threats of inflation and recession, Congress will feel the necessity of reducing the deficit and may cap Medicare expenditures. Past efforts to cap Medicare expenditures have been directed mainly at slowing the growth of fees paid to doctors. If limitations on fees become more severe, how will doctors react? Will many of them be able to refuse services to Medicare (and Medicaid) patients amounting to about a third of all fees paid to doctors? And what if they do? Another serious problem is the waste and fraud in the system. What regulations will be able to reduce that? Slowing the growth in the costs of Medicare will not be easy.

A second form of cost control might come through an insurance plan subsidized and administered by government to compete with private insurance companies. Such a government plan might have only a moderate restraint on cost, but it might also be revolutionary. The outcome would depend on the extent of government subsidies and how tightly the activities of the government plan are controlled.

The initial purpose of such a plan would be to provide competition to private insurance companies, forcing them to become more efficient and to limit profits. However, if government subsidies are substantial, the government plan could provide insurance at much lower prices than could private companies. Under the relentless pressure to cut health care costs, the government plan would likely undercut prices of private companies so far as to finally force them to drop health insurance. Government insurance would totally dominate the market. Such dominance would give it the power to set fees for providers, and we would have a health care system similar to those of other advanced countries. In all other advanced countries, government (or an agency of government) sets fees paid to doctors for each procedure performed. Those fees are typically about half the fees charged by doctors in the United States.

Another major cost saving would be in paper work in this government-dominated system. Costs would be cut by reducing present high billing costs, and the cost of justifying claims to insurance companies. Malpractice insurance costs would also be much lower, as they are today in government-run systems in other advanced countries.

In summary, a government-run health insurance plan that is tightly controlled and with limited subsidies would have only a moderate impact on reducing costs. But a heavily subsidized government-run insurance plan would have a major impact on reducing health care costs. It would also dramatically change many aspects of our health care system.

Step 10. An Alternative Approach

Before considering these harsh short-term price control systems, we should look ahead to a better long-term alternate health care system with more effective cost and quality controls.

Those three powerful forces described at the beginning of this section that are driving change in our health care system will be at least partially successful in attaining universal coverage, improving quality, and perhaps even slowing growth in costs. But we should hope for more. We can hope that a prestigious National Health Board, with members thoroughly qualified in medicine and science, and with a practical knowledge of the problems of delivering health care, would make a fundamental improvement in the nature of our health care system.

Most health care in the United States is delivered on a fee-for-service basis. Doctors and hospitals are paid a fee for each service rendered. This system invites doctors and hospitals to provide *more* services than necessary, *more elaborate, costly* services than necessary, and frequently to charge for services not even provided. Health care is burdened with waste and fraud. Extensive paper work is burdensome. Perhaps the National Health Board will move us gradually to a system where medical centers provide all medical services covered by that basic policy for an individual or a family for a monthly or yearly fee paid by insurance companies operating in a competitive insurance market. A medical center would have an incentive to eliminate waste, to use the most cost-effective procedures, to establish cooperative, low-cost relations with hospitals, and especially to emphasize preventive medicine and necessary lifestyle changes. Medical providers would have a great incentive to keep the patient well.

We should begin immediately to encourage this type of medical system. It is already used successfully by some prestigious medical centers such as the Cleveland Clinic and Kaiser Permanente. As Medicare and private insurance put more stringent limits on fees-for-service, doctors and other health care providers may be anxious to join a medical facility where they are paid by salary rather than working independently and realizing their income by fees-for-service. In ten years we might have many such medical centers competing with one another to offer the best services to patients at low cost. These medical centers would also compete with doctors and medical centers that continue to function as they do now. Insurance companies would be competing with each other to offer the most attractive *basic-plus* policies and to offer the lowest cost basic policies. The transition to the new system would be gradual, not disruptive.

The Nanny State, the Social Service of Last Resort

A capitalist democracy is based on individual responsibility. Each person should be responsible for his or her own welfare and for behavior that does not interfere with the rights of others. But some people fail to take this responsibility. They become wards of the nanny state. The prison system and the means-tested welfare system take control of, or help, those people who fail to take responsibility for their own behavior and welfare. A prisoner is in prison because some court has decreed that, at least for a time, he or she cannot be relied upon to assume personal responsibility. To become eligible for means-tested welfare, a person must prove that he or she does not have the assets or income to take responsibility for personal welfare.

The *prison population* in the United States increased around threefold from 1980 to the end of the century, and then leveled off. We may be able to hold the crime rate and the prison population down a little by education and by maintaining a very full employment economy, but the greatest need is to find a solution to the problem of illicit drugs. Drugs make people irresponsible. Crime is the ticket to the next fix. Violence is the ultimate method for settling disputes in the drug trade.

In a rapidly changing technological society such as ours, one might expect that a technical solution would be found. The human devastation of illicit drugs is so great that a large financial commitment is warranted if any technical approach appears to be promising.

The capitalist century will be a century of learning driven by competition. Few learning efforts hold the promise of a greater payoff than a vigorous effort to find a solution to the drug problem.

Means-tested welfare includes Medicaid, housing benefits, food benefits, Supplementary Security Income, and Temporary Assistance for Needy Families. The welfare rolls have been growing at a rapid rate, with expenditures rising from about 4 percent of all government outlays in 1968 to about 13 percent in 2002. Medicaid amounted to 63 percent of all welfare spending in 2002, so getting control of Medicaid costs is essential for getting control of the costs of means-tested welfare.

A conflict with ideological roots is the most interesting part of the debate on welfare policy. Presented as a *caricature*, it is a conflict between bleeding-heart liberals and tough-love conservatives (libertarians?). Bleeding-heart liberals press for greater aid to the unfortunate on humanitarian grounds to relieve hardship. This action is justified, they say, because poverty is often caused by faulty governments tolerating excessive unemployment, defective schools, and other impediments to a well-functioning society. Also, the unfortunate include many who have a poor genetic and nurturing heritage for which they are not responsible. Tough-love conservatives are concerned that welfare impairs incentives to work and save. Welfare destroys gumption. It creates dependency. Withholding welfare will spur people to work and prepare themselves for better jobs.

How has the conflict between putting emphasis on reducing hardship and putting emphasis on preserving incentives played out in recent history? In the late 1960s during the War on Poverty, requirements for getting welfare were eased to reduce hardship on the poor. Consequently, incentives to work were weakened. The number of people on welfare rose substantially in spite of the fact that business activity was increasing and job opportunities were improving. Then in the mid-1990s, to curb the growing cost of welfare, limitations were put on the period of time a person could receive welfare support. Incentives to work were thereby strengthened. The decline in welfare demands was startling. Rebecca Blank of the University of Michigan, describing the decrease in reliance on welfare as eligibility standards tightened, wrote, "Nobody of any political persuasion predicted or would have believed possible the magnitude of change that occurred in the behavior of low-income single-parent families over this decade."[12] A great deal of attention was recently paid to that tightening of welfare requirements as we passed its tenth anniversary. It is widely recognized as having been effective "tough love."

Reducing hardship on the poor by just handing out cash may be going out of style. When the poor need help, that help should, *as much as possible*, be tied to changes in behavior. That is, welfare payments should require changes in lifestyle. Recipients should be required to look for a job, take a job, get to work on time, get job training, go to school, keep children in school, and so on. Welfare should provide incentives for improvement and help in making improvement if it is to be effective. Requiring lifestyle changes is putting government in the position of monitoring much of the behavior of welfare recipients. That could make the government an *oppressive* nanny. It must be done with care.

Tough love has had some recent successes. But conservatives

should not get too complacent. We must not forget that people with defective genetic and nurturing heritage make up a large part of the poor. Considering their limited capabilities can they be driven to earn a decent living by government withdrawing welfare support? The requirement that lifestyles be changed in order to receive benefits must take into consideration the limited capabilities of those with below-average heritages.

The Earned Income Tax Credit described earlier is an excellent program. It has been expanded several times since inception because it helps relieve hardship on the poor while at the same time *increasing* incentives to work.

The No Child Left Behind program (although badly implemented) is another step in the right direction in that it is (in part) directed specifically at slow learners who often end up in the low part of the income brackets. We should do much more to test the limits of the techniques through which we can effectively help the slow learner.

But by far the best way to help those with defective heritage is by maintaining *very* full employment as described in this book, by better management of aggregate demand and structural competition.

Capitalist Social Services

In summary, the importance of capitalist social services can hardly be overstated. As described at the beginning of this chapter, social services have saved capitalism. They have mitigated the difficulties caused by capitalism's inevitable income inequality and therefore prevented the tearing apart of the social fabric that Greenspan fears will yet proceed from that inequality if it is not corrected.

Social services absorb such a large part of the output of capitalist countries that improving their efficiencies is mandatory.

Perhaps the trickiest part of improving social services will be to design policies that use tough love in dealing with people who simply lack gumption but also to have the flexibility to be more understanding in dealing with those who have a defective genetic and nurturing heritage.

Chapter 9

THE CAPITALIST IMPACT ON POPULATION

This chapter is short, but it is very important. It describes how capitalism will bring an end to the excessive population growth that has caused so many problems in recent decades and would bring disaster if continued long at past geometric rates. It also describes how the aging of America will impact Social Security and living standards.

An Environmentalist Dream That Will Come True

For decades the world's rising population has been considered by many to be a runaway juggernaut, soon to wreak havoc through overcrowding, famine, exhaustion of resources, and pollution. But things have changed. The end of population growth is now in sight. World population will likely grow from the present near 7 billion to a little more than 8 billion by midcentury. (The United Nations estimates that world population will peak at about 9 billion by midcentury.) That growth will still be a problem. Then it will level off and begin a powerful, long-lasting decline that will likely reduce it to significantly below its present size within the subsequent 100 years. A great deal of present-day farmland, not needed with smaller population and new technologies, will be abandoned and returned to nature. *The Economist* reported that the lynx and the wolf have already started returning to eastern Germany where population has been declining.[13]

This change in population trends was made probable in that period of awakening when many governments of *developing* countries began a major shift to capitalism, and several governments of *advanced* countries learned how to improve the capitalist system by controlling inflation without causing deep and long recessions, thus helping to ensure that capitalism will be copied. Following is the sequence of events that will dictate these new population trends:

• As capitalism spreads, attractive jobs by the billions are opening up in urban settings. Farmers, or their children, will leave the farm in favor of the more attractive urban life. Surely no one can believe that farmers or their children won't move as those attractive jobs become available. This is especially true in those vast areas where agriculture is mainly subsistence farming.

• When people move from the farm to urban settings, their fertility rates decline *sharply*. Children are a financial benefit on the farm in the form of low-cost labor. They are expensive to maintain in the city. Their cost is especially important when they make difficult a mother's working at a paid job outside the home. Furthermore, the urban environment is more conducive to women's education, use of contraceptives, divorce, abortion, and postponed marriages, all of which tend to reduce fertility rates.

• A fertility rate of 2.1 is the replacement rate that preserves a stable population. Two children are necessary to replace the parents. The 0.1 child is necessary to replace those who die before reaching the age of reproduction. The average fertility rate of advanced countries is now about 1.5. The average fertility rate of developing countries is about 3.0, having already dropped from 6.0 in the last few decades. No heroic assumptions are necessary to project a decline in the fertility rate of developing countries from 3.0 to 1.5 as people leave the farms where the majority of the people in those countries are now employed. A fertility rate of 1.5 means that the number of children born will decline by about one-quarter each *full* generation.

Perhaps the mothering instinct will rise to increase the fertility rate. Perhaps women will once again prefer large families over careers, automobiles, spacious homes, travel, entertainment, dogs, and cats. But it hasn't happened yet, and government pronatal efforts to increase fertility have seldom been effective. In the capitalist twenty-first century, over a billion people will likely leave the farms for the cities. A huge upsurge in mothering instinct will be required to offset that trend.

Environmentalists take note. The slowing of population growth, followed by an actual decline, can be speeded by facilitating the spread of capitalism that moves people to an urban setting.

Demographers often say *demography is destiny*, suggesting that the future of the human race depends on what happens to the population. *Knowledge is destiny*, is a more accurate projection of the future. The accumulation of knowledge has driven changes in demography. The abundance created by the accumulation of technical knowledge made possible the enormous increase in population of the last two centuries. Further technical development is creating even greater abundance, more attractive job opportunities, the need to live in cities, and the increased cost of raising children, thus slowing population growth. Those features, and many others, growing out of accumulated knowledge are the building blocks of our destiny. Much more will be said about the impact of knowledge accumulation in the final chapter.

Ben J. Wattenberg has recently written a book entitled *Fewer* that describes the declining fertility rates for several countries and regions.[14] It is an intriguing book containing implications for various aspects of life, power, and politics. It is a valuable resource for anyone interested in understanding the demographic trends that are helping to shape the world.

The Aging American Population

The world is getting older mainly because of the declining fertility rate. People are having fewer children, thus increasing the ratio of retired people to workers. In contrast to the other rich countries with sharply declining fertility rates, the fertility rate of the United States has remained nearly constant for over 15 years, just below the 2.1 percent replacement rate. America's high immigration rate accounts for part of the relatively high fertility rate. Immigrants and their children have a higher fertility rate than other Americans. Other factors are not clearly known, and a declining fertility rate may yet contribute to the aging of America.

A longer life span is the second cause of the aging of the world's population. That longer life span, of course, also contributes to the aging of America.

But a temporary factor will be especially important to the aging of America in the coming two decades. A 20-year baby boom following World War II is just now beginning to produce a large number of retired people. That baby boom was followed by a 25-year baby bust leading to a dearth of workers to support the growing band of retirees. The ratio of the number of retirees to the number of workers is called the dependency ratio. It is the major demographic feature we will have to deal with in the United States for the next two decades.

The Impact of Aging on Health Care and Social Security

The impact of aging on the cost of health care will be dramatic. The elderly have far greater medical needs than the young. Long-term care will be an especially difficult problem. The American health care system is already facing great difficulties. The aging problem will be a decisive blow that will force the changes described in Chapter 8.

As for Social Security, some people are worried that the system will be bankrupt by the time they retire. That view is far too pessimistic. Retirees in the next two or three decades will not receive *all* the Social Security benefits promised under present law, but they will receive most of them. If the law were to remain unchanged, retirees would receive presently promised benefits until 2037, at which time their benefits would drop to about three-quarters of the amount now promised. But the law will be changed. The retirement age will likely be postponed and monthly promised benefits will be slightly reduced to all but the lower-income retirees. Taxes may also be raised.

Since life expectancy will continue to expand, it is quite natural to expect people to retire at a later age. Under the present law, full retirement age is set to rise incrementally from 65 to 67 by 2027. The law will likely be changed so that the later retirement age of 67 will become effective before the year 2027.

Promised increases in monthly benefits will likely be reduced but only to the higher wage earners. One bill has been introduced in the Senate that would slow the growth of benefits to all but the lowest 30 percent of wage earners. The *initial* benefits paid to workers *at retirement* are currently rising as fast as average *wages*, which rise *faster* than the inflation rate. Under the proposed law, *initial* benefits for all but the lowest 30 percent of wage earners would increase only as fast as inflation. Benefits *after* the initial retirement date would increase at the inflation rate as they do now. This means that over the years, benefits of the upper 70 percent of wage earners would increase along with inflation instead of faster than inflation as they do now for *all* retirees.

Taxes may be raised instead of (or along with) slowing the growth of benefits. If they are raised, they will likely follow the pattern of the past, half to be paid by the worker and half by the employer. The tax on employers is based on the notion that they should bear half the burden. This is an illusion. In most cases the tax will be just another wage cost that must be passed on to the consumer in higher prices. The higher prices will bring the inflation rate a little closer to the ceiling that will cause the Federal Reserve to slow the economy, increasing unemployment. Or alternatively, the employer will slow the growth of wages, so the worker will bear the burden just as effectively as if the entire tax were levied upon him or her. This will especially be the case when the competitors are overseas and do not have to pay the tax.

Despite all the talk about Social Security going bankrupt, it is one of the easiest problems we have to solve. Improving our health care system and meeting the problems of people with a defective genetic and nurturing heritage will be far more difficult.

How Will the Aging of the Population Affect Living Standards?

Many people are worried that the coming rise in the number of retirees to be supported by the working population will slow the growth of our standard of living. The seriousness of that impact must be considered in relation to other factors that affect our economic well-being.

The aging of the population will certainly, by itself, slow growth of our living standards by reducing the proportion of the population at work. But not by much. In the coming 20 years, if all other factors were to remain unchanged, the increasing dependency ratio would *decrease* the growth of real GDP about one-half of one percent a year. But over the same period, output per hour worked (productivity) will *increase* about 2 percent a year, far more than offsetting the loss of production from the increasing dependency ratio. Furthermore, the retirement age will surely be raised as people live longer, offsetting a significant part of the rise in the dependency ratio.

Over the past half century, productivity has increased on average about 2 percent a year. I have projected that growth to continue for the coming 20 years. Is that realistic? Frequent arguments are heard that an older labor force will be less productive. That may be partly true, but I suggest that the intense worldwide competition that will prevail in the coming 20 years will keep productivity growth strong. Chapter 4 argued that productivity growth has an inverse relation to inflation. Both are largely determined by the intensity of competition. When competition is weak, inflation is high and productivity growth is slow. As Chapter 4 pointed out, those conditions existed in much of that inflation cycle from 1965 to 1990. Throughout this book I have argued that inflation will be kept under substantial control by structural and below-capacity competition. Inflation should average about 2-to-2.5 percent a year. If that projection materializes, productivity should continue to improve about 2 percent a year, or perhaps even more.

Technological change is a major force behind productivity improvements. The number of scientists probing nature's secrets will rise rapidly as advanced capitalism extends to the developing countries that contain 85 percent of the world's population. Scientific discovery is like a chain reaction. Every discovery stimulates other discoveries, which in turn stimulate further discoveries. The more scientists involved, the faster it grows. Knowledge accumulation could be explosive. The outlook for improved living standards in present-day advanced countries is good. For developing countries it is spectacular.

Chapter 10

CHOOSING AN INVESTMENT POLICY FOR THE CAPITALIST CENTURY

When you look at a long-term chart of U.S. stock prices, two facts stand out clearly. First, prices are in a long-term upward trend, and second, they fluctuate incessantly with no obviously recognizable pattern. An investment policy should take advantage of the upward trend and also protect against those incessant fluctuations, or better still, *profit* from those fluctuations.

First, the trend. In the second half of the twentieth century, stocks, as represented by the Standard and Poor 500 Average (S&P 500), rose to 84 times their beginning value. That was an annual growth rate of about 9 percent. In addition, stockholders received average annual dividends of about 3 percent, which (when reinvested in stock) raised the *total* annual return to about 12 percent. A thousand dollars invested in 1950 would have grown to an astonishing $290,000 by 2000, not deducting for income taxes. No wonder that many great fortunes were created during that period. In the first half of the capitalist twenty-first century, the S&P 500 will grow on average much more slowly, somewhere around an average annual rate of 5 percent or 11 times their beginning value in 50 years. That, plus reinvested dividends will provide a total appreciation of about 7 percent or 29 times their beginning value (not deducting for income taxes), still an attractive return. Later in this chapter I will show how that trend is estimated.

Second, those incessant fluctuations. They are treacherous. They raise the hopes of people struggling to increase their assets, only to shatter those hopes, sometimes quickly, sometimes in a long, grinding, down market. Fluctuations will still be with us in the capitalist century. At times they may appear to be worse. What policies will help to protect us against those fluctuations and even profit from them?

Two Forecasts

Following are two forecasts of financial market performance for the coming quarter century. The first assumes that Greenspan's grave fears about monetary policy (as described in Chapter 1) will be realized. Government will prevent the Federal Reserve from raising interest rates to contain coming inflation pressures. The second forecast is based on the arguments provided throughout this book, mainly that the Federal Reserve will do a reasonably effective job of stabilizing the inflation rate around 2-to-2.5 percent. The contrast between the two projections emphasizes the importance of the new, more reliable Federal Reserve policy for the future of the American economy.

If Greenspan's Fears Are Realized

If government succeeds in preventing the Federal Reserve from raising interest rates to contain inflationary forces, *economic predictability* will be shattered. Inflation will accelerate. Businessmen, consumers, and governments will come to expect faster and faster inflation. Interest rates will rise. Greenspan mentions a 10-percent rate on the 10-year Treasury note, over 3 times the present rate. The stock market will be erratic. Planning will be difficult. Growth will be slow. Unemployment will rise. Finally, inflation will become so severe that Federal Reserve restraint will be required to break that inflation, and we will face a serious recession as we did following the inflationary 1970s. We will live through a period of serious turbulence. Greenspan doesn't spell out all the problems that will follow a failure of the Federal Reserve to attack inflation early, but they are implicit in government action to prevent such intervention.

The present (early 2009) recession, as Chapter 5 described, is not a product of inflation, or of an effort to control inflation, but is a result of a failure to maintain the quality of credit in our banking system.

If the Federal Reserve Maintains a Reliable Inflation-Restraint Policy

A successful Federal Reserve policy that keeps inflation within that 2-to-2.5 percent range most of the time will have an enormously beneficial impact on many aspects of the economy, not the least of which is to improve the ability to forecast the trend of stock prices and to help determine when stocks are overpriced and underpriced. This chapter explores how this is done.

A vast spending-income stream flows through the economy. Spending generates income, which generates more spending, which generates more income, repeated over and over again. The Department of Commerce estimates that flow of dollars and reports it every quarter. It is called the nominal Gross Domestic Product (GDP). *The earnings of the S&P 500 have shown a growth trend for many years nearly the same as that of the nominal GDP.* So if we can predict the trend of the nominal GDP we have a good chance of predicting the trend of S&P 500 earnings and S&P 500 stock prices.

Variations in the inflation rate have been the major factor that has caused wide variations in the growth trend of nominal GDP in the last half century. If the Federal Reserve succeeds in stabilizing the growth of the inflation rate, it will also stabilize the growth trend of the nominal GDP and the S&P 500 earnings and enable us to better predict the growth trend of stock prices.

Also, the inflation rate is the major factor in determining the long-term interest rate. *So if the Federal Reserve stabilizes the inflation rate, it will also stabilize long-term interest rates.* Comparing the more stable long-term interest rates with the more predictable earnings of stocks will help to determine when stocks are overpriced and underpriced.

Therefore, predictability and financial planning depend very much on how we judge the ability and willingness of the Federal Reserve to stabilize the inflation rate. The following detailed projections for the coming 25 years are derived from the conviction that the Federal Reserve will hold the inflation rate *most of the time* close to that 2-to-2.5 percent range. The rest of the chapter justifies these projections.

• The inflation premium part of interest rates will gradually settle near the 2-to-2.5 percent inflation rate. *Real* interest rates (the other part) will likely rise, probably to about 2.5 to 3 percent, producing an approximate 5 percent (4.5-to-5.5) average interest rate on the 10-year Treasury notes. Long-term interest rates (and bond prices) will fluctuate far less widely than they have in the past as the Federal Reserve's credibility becomes more firmly established. A better predictability of the future value of the dollar will be achieved. Planning and risk appraisal will be improved.

• Growth of *nominal* GDP will average about 5 percent, consisting of 2-to-2.5 percent inflation and 2.5-to-3 percent *real* growth. The real growth is determined by the growth of hours worked and the output per hour (productivity). A 2.5-to-3 percent real growth rate is considerably slower than the 3.4 percent annual growth of the last century. The labor force will likely grow more slowly. Greenspan projects real growth at about 2.5 percent. The growth of *nominal* GDP will be far less erratic than in the period before the awakening because inflation will be far less erratic. That growth will, of course, still be affected by recessions.

• Earnings on the S&P 500 stock average will grow at about the same average rate as *nominal* GDP, about 5 percent.

• The stock market (at 700 on the S&P 500 in early 2009) will nearly triple in the coming 3 to 5 years.

There are huge differences between these projections and the turbulence to be expected if Greenspan's fears are realized. Federal Reserve inflation-control policies are critical. They are an important key to an age of *declining* turbulence. More people are learning that fact. Justifications for the above projections follow throughout this chapter.

Interest Rates

What determines the bond interest rate? It has two parts: first, the *real* interest rate, which is a payment to the lender for the use of the money over the life of the loan, and second, the inflation premium that protects the lender against loss in the value of the principal during the life of the loan. The inflation premium was by far the most volatile part of the interest rate in the second half of the twentieth century.

Chart 10.1 shows three twentieth century inflation surges indicated by the vertical shaded areas. The first two were related to the world wars and their aftermaths. The third surge accompanied the Vietnam War and continued several years after the war. It was also exacerbated by the oil shocks. That inflation surge was *not* mainly a result of the war or the oil shocks but

Chart 10.1 Interest Rates on 10-Year Treasury Note (Annual Averages) Inflation Surges (Shaded Areas)

Source: R. Shiller, "From Efficient Markets Theory to Behavioral Finance," J. Econ. Pers. 2003; *Market Volatility*; *Irrational Exuberance*

rather of a *relaxation of Federal Reserve anti-inflation policies.* Inflation began to accelerate eight years *before* the first oil shock. The lack of inflation restraint was partly a result of pressure from the administration and partly a product of the advice of some economists who believed that unemployment could be permanently lowered by allowing faster inflation. (A fascinating account of the arguments and struggles leading to the critical decision to modify inflation controls can be found in a recent book, *Chairman of the Fed* by Robert P. Bremner.[15]) We have learned much about inflation, and in coming decades, control of inflation will be far better than in twentieth century capitalism's defective childhood. Mainly we have learned that inflation must be attacked early before it becomes well established.

Inflation drives up interest rates as lenders demand an inflation premium to pay for the risk that the money will lose value by the time it is repaid. Chart 10.1 also shows how long-term United States Treasury interest rates were affected by the inflation surges. Interest rates rose in the World War I surge but not in World War II. In that second inflation surge, Treasury interest rates were pegged at a low level by the Federal Reserve to aid the war effort. After the controls were lifted, suppressed forces were released and drove interest rates up substantially. Interest rates rose dramatically in the

149

third inflation surge. Several years passed after the inflation surge ended before investors lost their fears of another bout of inflation, gradually allowing interest rates to decline.

The inflation of 1965-80 was not nearly as great a catastrophe as were the two world wars and the Great Depression. But it was not a happy time. The rampant inflation raised fears that it could not be stopped without triggering another Great Depression with a possible end to democracy. Yet it could not be allowed to continue for fear of triggering hyperinflation with its inevitable breakdown. Inflation fears were accentuated by the cultural revolution, the Cold War, gasoline shortages, Watergate, high unemployment, high interest rates, and slow economic growth. The country seemed to be in danger of falling apart.

Real interest rates vary with the changing supply of and demand for loanable funds. Both demand for and supply of loanable funds are impacted by consumers, businesses, and governments. The consumer savings rate, business financial policies, and the amount of government deficit financing are all critical in determining the real interest rate. More and more, real interest rates are determined on a worldwide basis. In the past decade the government has sold Treasury Inflation Protected Securities (TIPS). Since the interest rate and principal are protected against loss from inflation, the yield is a rough approximation of the *real* interest rate. TIPS are relatively new and have less liquidity than other Treasury securities. Their yield is therefore not a *precise* measure of the real interest rate. The yield on TIPS has varied between 2 and 4 percent.

Adjusting for that lack of liquidity of TIPS, one might estimate the *real* interest rate to have been in the neighborhood of 2 percent. Real interest rates in the future will be impacted by declining personal savings rates in developing countries, by possible rising savings rates in the United States and elsewhere as the home mortgage bubble winds down, by changes in fiscal policies of governments around the world, by the need for vast amounts of capital to improve the world's infrastructure and protect against global warming, and by dozens of other factors. My judgment is that real interest rates will rise and *average* about 2.5-to-3 percent in the coming quarter century. That rate plus an inflation premium of about 2-to-2.5 percent should produce an average interest rate of about 4.5-to-5.5 percent on 10-year Treasury notes. The current (early-2009) yield of 2.75 percent on the ten-year note is unusually low. Rates below 4 percent will likely not often be seen in the coming half century. More about this later. The interest rate is important in determining stock values.

Growth of Nominal GDP

Nominal GDP has two parts: the real output of goods and services and the prices of those goods and services.

Chart 10.2 shows *real* GDP since 1900. It shows a strong upward trend of 3.4 percent. (A straight line on a ratio scale indicates a constant rate of growth.) Major fluctuations around that trend were mainly a result of the onset of, and recovery from, the Great Depression. The growth rate of real output is determined by the growth rate in hours worked plus the change in output per hour worked—productivity. The growth rate in the number of hours worked will likely slow thanks to the increasing percentage of the population that will be retired, and a slowing growth in the number of women entering the labor force. The growth rate of real output has, therefore, been projected at a moderately slower 2.5-to-3

Chart 10.2 Real GDP Index (1900=100)

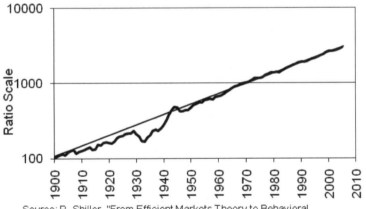

Source: R. Shiller, "From Efficient Markets Theory to Behavioral Finance," J. Econ. Pers. 2003; *Market Volatility; Irrational Exuberance*

percent. The Federal Reserve is expected to peg the inflation rate at about 2-to-2.5 percent. Adding that to the expected real growth rate of 2.5-to-3 percent gives a growth rate of about 5 percent (4.5-to-5.5) for *nominal* GDP.

Earnings on the S&P 500 Stock Index

What then is the outlook for S&P 500 earnings growth? The long-term trend in its growth rate is reasonably close to the long-term trend in the growth rate of nominal GDP. The S&P 500 index averages the stock prices of 500 of the largest corporations in the United States. Each of those large corporations is striving by sales efforts to extract as many dollars as possible from the huge spending-income-spending stream flowing through the economy. The nominal GDP is a measure of that stream. Furthermore, those 500 companies are trying to make those sales with the highest possible profit margin. It is not unreasonable to believe that their average success in achieving those desired sales and earnings goals will be roughly the same in the coming quarter century as they were under similar conditions that prevailed in the previous quarter century. In that quarter century, S&P 500 earnings grew at almost exactly the same average rate as nominal GDP. S&P 500 earnings should continue to grow on average at about the same rate as nominal GDP in the coming quarter century, about 5 percent a year. Also, in the inflationary 1970s, S&P 500 earnings grew at about the same rate as nominal GDP under far different conditions. So for the last 35 years, the S&P 500 earnings growth trend matched the growth trend of nominal GDP.

Going back even farther, the two trends differ somewhat, but for understandable reasons. In the first three decades of the twentieth century up to the beginning of the Great Depression, the growth rate of S&P 500 earnings was a little more than half the growth rate of nominal GDP. That slower earnings growth rate can largely be explained by the high dividend payout ratio compared with that of recent decades. Paying out higher dividends left a smaller proportion of earnings to fuel future growth. In those two terrible decades of the Great Depression and World War II (and aftermath), growth in S&P 500 earnings was less than half that of nominal GDP. Again the low growth rate, compared to the growth rate of nominal GDP, coincided with a very high payout ratio. The next 20 years, from the end of World War II to the beginning of the 1970s inflation decade, witnessed S&P 500 earnings growth somewhat more than half the growth rate of nominal GDP. Much of that slower S&P 500 earnings growth rate can also be accounted for by a high payout ratio. So even the very long-term record is reasonably suggestive of the idea that the S&P 500 earnings trend will match the probable 5-percent growth trend of nominal GDP in the coming quarter century.

The New Investment World

We live in a new investment world. Of all the factors we have examined that will distinguish the future performance of stock prices, the more-constant inflation rate represents by far the greatest change from the pre-awakening period. And that, of course, depends on whether Greenspan's worries are realized. Look back at that important Chart 10.1. If government prevents the Federal Reserve from raising short-term interest rates to restrain inflation as Greenspan so greatly fears, we are in for another inflation episode with wild changes in long-term interest rates as prevailed between 1965 and the mid-1990s. Now visualize that interest rate line extending far into the future with only a point or two variation around the 5 percent average. That will be a striking change in the investment environment. As expectations of better inflation control become more firmly established, we will indeed live in a new investment world.

Remember the 1970s? Oil prices quadrupled. The Vietnam War dragged on. The CPI inflation rate peaked at about 15 percent. Even the core inflation rate peaked at nearly 15 percent. It also remained above 6 percent for a decade.

Now look at our recent inflation. Oil prices quadrupled. The Iraq and Afghanistan wars dragged on. The CPI inflation rate peaked at about 6 percent (not 15 percent). The core inflation rate peaked at about 3 percent (not 15 percent) and averaged only about 2.5 percent (not over 6 percent) after the oil price surge began. Furthermore, the recent inflation rate has also been aggravated by a sharp rise in food prices and complicated by the most serious financial crisis since the Great Depression. That is a fairly persuasive bit of anecdotal evidence that the inflation-control world has changed.

Another part of this new investment world should be emphasized. Improved inflation control automatically improves recession control. By far the most severe recessions the United States has suffered since the Great Depression were the two recessions that followed efforts by the Federal Reserve to control inflation *after it had become well established* in the 1970s. The first, in 1975, increased unemployment to about 9 percent, and the second, an intermittent recession from 1980 to 1982, increased the unemployment rate to about 11 percent. Before those two recessions, unemployment had peaked at 7 percent *or less* in recessions. By attacking inflation early we will reduce the danger of serious recession but not entirely eliminate it. The current recession, a product of the subprime mortgage crisis, may be very large if not attacked boldly.

This book has argued that other events that occurred during the awakening, beginning about 1980, have also changed the investment world. The ongoing, worldwide extension of capitalism and more extensive international trade have increased the structural competition that helps keep inflation under control, requiring less Federal Reserve restraint, as described in Chapter 4. Worldwide capitalism will also keep productivity growth high. We are learning how to better use fiscal policy as a support for monetary policy to mitigate recessions. The subprime mortgage fiasco has probably taught us the necessity of preserving the quality of credit by simple regulation at the point where the credit is granted, as described in Chapter 5. Yes, we are living in a different, and better, investment world. But one important problem for investors will still remain. Substantial fluctuations in stock prices will be part of this new investment world. Sometimes stocks will be overpriced, sometimes underpriced.

An Approach to Estimating a "Normal" Value for Stocks

Stocks cannot be valued in isolation. The value of stocks depends in part on the value of alternative investments to which the investor can turn. Few alternative investments are available.

We will compare stock investment with only one—long-term bond investment, the major alternative to stocks. The 10-year Treasury note will be used to represent the universe of bonds, and the S&P 500 stock index to represent the universe of stocks.

High returns on bonds affect the price of stocks because many investors shift their investment funds between stocks and bonds. High returns on bonds tend to draw funds away from stock investment and thus hold down the price of stocks. The difficulty comes in estimating when the *expected* returns on stocks are better or worse than the *expected* return on bonds. That judgment has to be made on a risk-adjusted basis. How can that comparison between expected returns on bonds and stocks be made?

We can best illustrate the problems of appraising the comparative investment merits of bonds and stocks by examining the early 2009 investment problem faced by investors. By the time this book is published, interest rates and stock prices will likely have changed substantially. Nevertheless the following analysis will provide a useful procedure for comparing stock and bond investment.

In early 2009, the 10-year Treasury note is trading at a price that provides an interest return of about 2.75 percent. If an investor buys a 10-year Treasury note today, he will buy an annual interest return of $2.75 for each $100 invested. That 2.75-percent rate will be locked in for 10 years.

If the investor buys the S&P 500 stock average at its present 700 price with *estimated* operating earnings of $40 for 2009, he will buy an *earnings* yield (not *dividend* yield) of 5.7 percent ($40 divided by 700). He will buy $5.70 of *current* earnings for each $100 invested. The current earnings yield on stocks is much higher than the $2.75 interest return on bonds. But that is only a part of the 2009 comparison of bond and stock investment. These returns are affected by the slow business environment. They are transitory. They are not normal.

An investor buying a 10-year 2.75-percent Treasury note is paying more than a normal price. As described earlier, the normal interest is about 5 percent. As business activity recovers and the market rate of interest rises toward that normal 5 percent, the market price of the investor's bond with an interest rate of only 2.75 percent will *decline* and remain below his purchase price until maturity.

What does the stock investor get for his $100? Estimated operating earnings on the S&P 500 for 2009 are only about $40. *But if the economy were operating near full capacity,* earnings would be about $90, an earnings yield of 13 percent on the S&P 500 trading at 700. So he is buying stocks with a 2009 *latent earning power* of 13 percent. This normal (full employment) earnings yield on stocks is far greater than the 5 percent normal (full employment) interest return on bonds. A long-term investor should buy stocks on the basis of *latent earning power*. He should *not* buy them on the basis of current earnings.

How are the *normal* earnings (latent earning power) on the S&P 500 estimated? Chart 10.3 shows *operating* earnings accruing to the S&P 500 index beginning in 1988. The year 1988 is a valid starting point because by that time the economy and the stock market had largely recovered from the inflationary 1970s and aftermath. Earnings fluctuated widely between 1988 and 2008, dropping in recessions when profit margins were driven down by below-

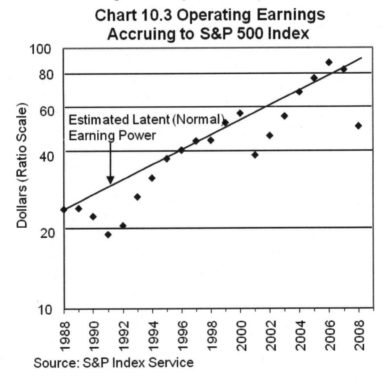

Chart 10.3 Operating Earnings Accruing to S&P 500 Index

Source: S&P Index Service

156

capacity competition. In a few cases when output was pressing strongly against capacity limits, competition was weak and profit margins were excessive. The operating earnings shown in this chart were *actual* earnings, not *normal* earnings. *Earnings are considered normal only when the economy is operating just below full capacity.*

The trend line shown on Chart 10.3 passes through (or is close to) the earnings of the S&P 500 for each year when the unemployment rate was at or near 5 percent, considered to be just under full employment. We can, therefore, interpolate from that trend line what the earnings would likely have been for other years if the economy had been operating at 5 percent unemployment. That is, the trend line estimates latent earning power *for each year*. In addition, it shows that the growth trend during that 20 year period was almost two percentage points higher than the 5 percent I have projected for nominal GDP and S&P 500 earnings for the coming years. The chart also shows the substantial difference between latent earning power and actual earnings in 2008.

The stock investor buying the S&P 500 at 700 gets much more than that $90 latent earning power for 2009 with latent earnings yield of 13 percent. Latent earning power will grow on average at about 5 percent a year along with nominal GDP. Over time, that increase in latent earning power will be matched by a similar appreciation in the market price trend of stocks. That appreciation, by itself, is equivalent to the normal 5-percent interest return on bonds. In addition the stock investor gets a cash dividend each year amounting to one-fourth to one-third of those growing earnings. And the stock investor has a tax advantage. The stock investor does not have to pay taxes on his gain through stock appreciation until he sells the stock. That postponement of the tax is a huge advantage. Furthermore, the gain is taxed at a lesser capital-gain rate, which is currently much lower than the tax rate on ordinary income. The rewards of stock investment at early-2009 appear to be far superior to the rewards of bond investment.

Stock investment requires a risk adjustment, which is a disadvantage to stock ownership. The prices of stocks fluctuate incessantly over wide ranges. Investors who may need their money within a few years find difficulty in facing the uncertainty of those fluctuations. Furthermore, those fluctuations include possible deep market declines resulting from adverse expectations of inflation, recession, war, and shocks such as a flu pandemic and the recent subprime mortgage crisis. Those risks must be evaluated. They cannot be ignored. That is what this book is all about. With its emphasis on what we have learned and the worldwide extension of capitalism, it provides a justification for an age of declining turbulence.

Valuing Stocks by Using Latent Earning Power

Stocks should be valued on the basis of latent earning power because the economy is expected to return to full employment reasonably soon, at which time that latent earning power will be realized. Those who believe that we have not learned a great deal about managing a capitalist economy will be reluctant to accept that view and will be reluctant to base their stock valuations on latent earning power.

How much will investors pay for that latent earning power in the next 25 years? Let's look at the record. Between 1955 and 1970 the S&P 500 traded most of the time between 14 and 17 times estimated latent earning power. That period experienced good economic growth interrupted only by small recessions. But when the inflationary 1970s arrived, investors refused to reward growing latent earning power. Nominal GDP, the source of S&P 500 earnings, was growing both through rising output and inflation. The multiple of latent earning power dropped, and the market remained stagnant for a decade between 1975 and 1985. The S&P 500 traded between 7 and 9 times latent earning power. This is the kind of performance we can expect in the coming years if the Federal Reserve is prevented by government from raising interest rates to control inflation, as Greenspan fears.

As the economy healed following the 1970s inflation and recession aftermath, stock prices improved, and the S&P 500 traded in the first half of the 1990s mostly between 12 and 14 times latent earning power. Then speculation took hold, and the S&P 500 climbed to over 25 times latent earning power. After the crash, stocks steadied and traded for 5 years between 14 and 17 times latent earning power until the subprime mortgage banking crisis arrived. At 700 in early 2009, it is trading at less than 8 times latent earning power. The optimistic analysis of this book leads me to believe that the S&P 500 will trade most of the time in the range of 15 to 20 times latent earning power in the coming 25 years. It will do so only if my contention that we have learned a great deal about managing a capitalist economy is correct.

A Brief History of the Risks
and Rewards of Stock Investment

The underlying tension in the stock market between the risks of stock ownership and the rewards of stock ownership will continue. A brief historical review will help by showing how that tension has played out in the past.

At the beginning of the twentieth century, stocks were considered to be too risky to qualify as investment grade. Only bonds were investments. Stocks were speculations. That perception changed only gradually until the 1920s, when stocks were finally admitted to the investment club. Then their superior financial performance brought widespread ownership. Stock prices tripled in less than a decade, culminating in the speculative orgy of 1929.

The Great Depression destroyed the perception of the investment quality of stocks. Risk was again emphasized. In 1933 the average price of the S&P 500 was almost identical to its average price in 1902. (Annual averages of stock prices are used in these comparisons.) Thirty-one years of accumulated investment value were wiped out. Those who believe we have not learned a great deal about managing a capitalist economy should take note. Unless we have learned much about managing capitalism, that destruction of stock values could happen again through the recurrence of depression or inflation.

From 1933 to 1937 stocks more than doubled in price as the perception of risk diminished. But the 1937-38 recession and the onset of World War II revived worries about the investment quality of stocks. After Pearl Harbor the price of stocks dropped in 1942 to their 1933 low, which, of course, was also the level of 1902, 40 years earlier.

Recovery after World War II was substantial. The S&P 500 rose elevenfold in the 27 years from 1942 to 1969. Memories of war and depression faded. Confidence in the survival and growth of capitalism in the face of the communist threat grew even though the Cold War persisted.

Then, under relaxed Federal Reserve anti-inflation policies, the unhappy inflationary 1970s arrived. Emphasis on risk mounted, and stocks ended the decade near where they started the decade.

In the late 1970s and early 1980s Paul Volcker, newly appointed chairman of the Federal Reserve Board, stabilized the United States economy by aggressive monetary restraint and set it on course for two decades of magnificent noninflationary growth. Volcker kept to the anti-inflation course in spite of vicious criticism. Greenspan reports that one congressman told Volcker that he was high on the list of candidates for lynching thanks to the restrictive actions he had taken to break the inflation. But Volcker was right. America owes a lot to his wisdom and courage. From the end of the 1970s to the end of the century, in just 20 years, stocks rose thirteenfold, culminating in the late 1990s speculative bubble.

The breaking of that speculative bubble together with the recession, the shock of 9/11, the spike in oil prices, wars in Iraq and Afghanistan, and the fears of another recession constrained stock prices for several years. Risk was emphasized, and the rising value of latent stock earning power was passed over.

Two observations should be made about the shift in attention paid to the risks and rewards of stock investment: First, as time passes following a catastrophe such as the Great Depression or a somewhat lesser difficulty such as the inflationary 1970s, memories fade and investors worry less about risk and pay more attention to the growing earning power of stocks. The same thing will happen as we get farther and farther away from the subprime mortgage debacle. The risks of stock ownership will gradually fade from memory, and the potential rewards of stock ownership will become more alluring. Second, a stock investor today is betting a great deal on the assumption that we have learned much about the management of a capitalist economy. If it turns out that we have forgotten the lessons we learned the hard way by making, and correcting, mistakes, stocks do not have nearly the appreciation potential projected in this chapter.

The Current, Early 2009, Economic Outlook

President Obama, Congress, and the Federal Reserve will be under intense pressure to bring the unemployment rate down from the double-digit level where it will likely peak, to a more tolerable 5 percent. The voting public quite properly holds government responsible for maintaining full employment. If economic activity remains sluggish, and unemployment remains high as the 2010 congressional election looms closer, we will surely see additional, aggressive fiscal stimulus initiatives and strong Federal Reserve monetary support. Pressures will be even greater as we approach the 2012 election.

The United States has all but one of the requirements needed to bring unemployment down to 5 percent in two or three years. We have, or will have, the labor force and plant and equipment necessary to produce the goods to satisfy the increased demand that will bring that unemployment rate down to 5 percent. We probably have sufficiently-intense structural competition to keep inflation under control at a 5 percent unemployment rate for at least a year or two. The banking system is now reasonably stable. The one missing item is adequate demand. Government has the responsibility of creating demand by increasing spending (including stimulative payments to consumers), cutting taxes, and completing the rehabilitation of our financial system. Fear of increased budget deficits from another stimulus package will likely be gradually moderated by the growing realization that the deficit will be almost as large (perhaps larger) in a long drawn-out recession without the stimulus as it would be with the stimulus. Both economic growth and tax revenue would be sharply lower without the stimulus.

To bring unemployment down, government and the Fed must increase GDP enough to offset its recession-induced decline and then keep it growing at about a 5 percent rate. S&P 500 earnings will follow. Of course, I must once again raise the inflation issue. As inflation accelerates, threatening to rise above the Federal Reserve target rate, it will be promptly attacked. Since that restraint will come early, it will be mild. The slowing of the economy will also be mild.

The Current, Early 2009, Stock Market Outlook

Estimated latent earning power of the S&P 500 is $90 for 2009. Remember, latent earning power is the amount that the S&P 500 would earn if the economy were operating just below full employment. This latent earning power will grow at an average compound rate of 5 percent a year as it continues to match the 5 percent growth *trend* of nominal GDP.

As indicated earlier, I suggest that in the coming 25 years the price of the S&P 500 stock index will gravitate toward a central zone bounded by a 20 multiple of *latent earning power* at the top and a multiple of 15 at the bottom. That zone, I believe, is the approximate range that investors will come to recognize as providing a proper balance between the risks and rewards of stock ownership in the *improving world economy* of the coming 25 years. In 2009, 1800 is the top of the zone and 1350 the bottom, based on $90 latent earning power.

Even if a long-term investor buys the S&P 500 at a 20 multiple of latent earning power (at the top of the zone), he will be rewarded with a compound gain of 5 percent on his investment over a long period as stock prices match average earning gains. He will also receive cash dividends of about 2 to 3 percent of the market value of his stocks each year, and, of course, he will have a huge tax advantage on his stock appreciation. He will have to suffer the risk (pain) of wide fluctuations in the market value of his investment. That pain will become extreme if he is hit with an unexpected need for his funds, turning him into a short-term investor. Purchases of the S&P 500 even at the top of the zone will be better for a long-term investor than buying long-term Treasury bonds yielding less than 5 percent.

A long-term investor who buys the S&P 500 at the present price of 700 gets that 5 percent growth in latent earning power, dividends, and tax advantage. In addition he gets an appreciation potential of more than 100 percent just to bring the stock price up to 1575, the center of that rising target zone. He is buying the S&P 500 at a time of intense fear, fear of an even more severe collapse of our banking system and the depression (not recession) that that collapse would likely engender.

A long-term investor who bought the S&P 500 at the average trading price of 1425 in the year 2000, about 25 times the estimated latent earning power, well above that target zone, now has a 50 percent loss on his investment, but can look forward to recovering most of that loss within the next two or three years and also reaping a considerable gain in the years that follow. He also has collected cash dividends for nearly a decade, which, if invested in the S&P 500 at the time of receipt, has lowered the average cost of his less-than-prudent purchase made at a time of rampant speculation.

Stock prices will continue to fluctuate widely within and around that designated target zone. At times after long periods of noninflationary growth, investors will view the future through the distorting lens of greed and, swayed by the madness of crowds, will drive stock prices to unrealistic heights. In 2000, for example, stock prices were so high that the yield on latent earning power had dropped to 3.5 percent. That was 1.5 percentage points *below* the normal bond interest rate of 5 percent.

At times of considerable difficulty as in the years since 2000, investors will view the future through the distorting lens of fear, and swayed by the madness of crowds, will drive stock prices down to unrealistic lows. The S&P 500 at the present price of 700 at early 2009 has an estimated latent earnings yield of 13 percent, based on $90 estimated latent earning power, nearly 8 percentage points *above* the normal bond yield.

Even if this bear market has somewhat farther to run, and even though recovery from the recession takes three to four years, life will still go on for the long-term investor. Buying the S&P 500 at current prices will, in the end, prove to have been far better than buying long-term Treasury bonds.

Note to readers: Part of these projections, such as the relationship between the nominal GDP and S&P 500 earnings, are based on objective evidence, but other parts are more subjective, based on the analyses of the forces driving improvements in world capitalism as described throughout this book.

Short-Term Investment

So much money can be made by correctly forecasting short-term market movements that a great many people keep trying. Some people do it fairly well. A few do it very well. But to most it is a beguiling money trap. A short-term trader has to forecast economic and political events. Even worse, he has to forecast how other investors will react to these events. Forecasts of short-term investor behavior are difficult to make.

The relationship between the earnings yield on stocks and the interest rate on bonds is sometimes useful as a predictive device for short-term forecasters, but it is used in a different way than it has been used in this chapter. For long-term investors, we have compared the *normal* earnings yield (latent earnings yield) to the *normal* interest rate. For short-term forecasting the *current* earnings yield on stocks is compared to the *current* interest rate on the 10-year Treasury note. Much of the time in the past quarter century the two have moved quite closely together and have been a useful predictive device. When they have diverged, they have come back together again within a year or two—that is, until 2002. Since then the earnings yield has been 2 percentage points or more above the bond interest rate. Investors have been reluctant to pay high enough prices for stocks to bring the yield down to the bond interest-rate level. This caution on the part of stock buyers has probably been a reaction to the losses suffered in the collapse of the turn-of-the-century stock market bubble. Also 9/11, the Iraq war, the oil price spike, and the beginning of another recession have added to that caution. Optimism will probably soon return, and that earlier relationship between current stock yields and current bond interest rates will likely return with it, making it again a useful short-term predictive device. The relationship between current bond interest and current stock yields cannot be used alone for short-term forecasts. It must be accompanied by market analysis (psychology), monetary analysis, and economic analysis in general.

Mechanical Investment Plans

This brief discussion of short-term investment cannot end without describing two time-tested mechanical plans for dealing with those pesky short-term fluctuations. The plans require only one forecast—that the economy will continue to grow most of the time. Millions of people have built sizable retirement accounts by using a simple investment policy—*dollar cost averaging*. Buy a specified dollar amount of stock each month as in a payroll deduction plan. You buy more *shares* when prices are low than when prices are high, so your *average* cost is reasonable, and you profit from the trend. You are protected from buying only when conditions seem favorable (and prices are high) and selling, or failing to buy, when the environment is gloomy (and prices are low).

A dollar cost averaging plan works well for someone with a fairly regular stream of income. A *balanced-fund* approach works for someone with an existing fund needing investment. The balanced fund requires no more forecasting ability than the dollar cost averaging approach. The fund is divided into two parts. Half is invested in bonds, and the other half in stocks. If stocks rise to the point where they amount to more than 60 percent of the fund, stocks are sold and the money invested in bonds, keeping the stock share below 60 percent. If stocks decline so their share of the fund is below 40 percent, bonds are sold and the money invested in stocks, bringing their share of the fund up to 40 percent. This plan forces the investor to buy stocks *after* they have declined and to sell them *after* they have risen. Many variations on this plan can be designed by using different proportions of bonds and stocks. (Index funds are used in both of these well-known mechanical plans to avoid the necessity of forecasting the outlook for individual companies. Both plans are reliable only when they can be continued for several years. Neither of the plans will be as profitable in the coming half century as they were in the second half of the twentieth century because stock prices will not rise as fast.)

Even these mechanical plans require a long-term view of the future. If you anticipate a period of serious inflation with interest rates in double digits, as Greenspan fears, you must be prepared for a possible extended period of losses under either mechanical plan. That would test your resolve and might lead you to abandon the plan at just the wrong time. Even the present recession is testing the resolve of users of mechanical plans. Those who continue their plans should reap substantial rewards.

Chapter 11

THE CAPITALIST CENTURY AND BEYOND

Our achievements in the twenty-first century will depend to a great extent on how much we have learned about managing a capitalist economy. I am now 91 years old. I remember vividly the Great Depression with unemployment that topped out at 25 percent, remained above 20 percent for four years and above 10 percent for ten years. I remember World War II as viewed from the deck of a destroyer escort in the South Pacific, the not-so-little Korean War with its 54,000 American casualties, and the not-so-little Vietnam War with its 58,000 American casualties. I remember the long Cold War and those movies that portrayed the horrible consequences of a nuclear exchange. I remember the dozens of long-lasting, but pathetic, struggles to make government-managed economies work in stagnant countries around the world. And I remember the 1970s inflation with its fears of pending disaster. I cannot possibly believe that our performance this last quarter century represents anything but a substantial learning victory. Its benefits should continue to unfold.

The last third of my 91 years has witnessed the extraordinary spread of capitalism around the world. I must believe that that expansion is a result of the three powerful forces described in this book:

• The lure of capitalist abundance propels governments to turn to capitalism and generally stay on course for its improvement. Most people and governments really crave that abundance.

• Competition among governments to attract capital investment is *driving*, and will continue to drive, governments toward policies necessary for prosperity, civil liberties, and peace.

• The growing variety of goods required in a developing capitalist economy *demands* ever-expanding trading areas to find the specialists that can produce those goods efficiently. The increased interdependence has put us firmly on the pathway toward world peace. Time is on the side of peace.

Viewed from the depths of the recession caused by the subprime mortgage debacle, we tend to be gloomy. But after the recession ends we will look back on that debacle as a learning experience. We will not likely ever again accept the view that the financial markets can regulate themselves. Our accumulated knowledge of how to manage a capitalist economy, gained the hard way by making (and correcting) mistakes, will more and more be seen as a precious treasure to pass on to our children. They will have the challenge of continuing to add to that knowledge.

Capitalism's Impact on Human Behavior

If you doubt the power of capitalist abundance and freedom of choice to change human behavior in the twenty-first century, stop a moment to reflect on this fact: Capitalism has already dramatically weakened one of the most powerful forces that has driven human behavior for millennia—the *desire to procreate*. As indicated in Chapter 9, capitalist abundance and freedom of choice have already replaced large families with careers, spacious homes, cars, travel, entertainment, dogs, and cats. A force that powerful must command attention. What other aspects of human behavior will capitalism change in the twenty-first century and beyond?

Capitalist abundance and freedom of choice have already spawned a wave of *gluttony* (overindulgence in food and drink). Obesity is a growing problem. Alcohol and drug abuse are part of the package. Gluttony is one of the widely cited "seven deadly sins," a conceptual grouping that has spread from its base in the teachings of the early Christian church. The impact of capitalist abundance on this temptation is obvious. My curiosity was aroused, so I decided to try to determine what impact capitalism is having on the other six deadly sins.

Judging from America's movies and television programming, *lust* has been a major beneficiary of capitalist abundance and freedom of choice. It has been happily welcomed by many. Others feel that it is a major factor behind the breakup of the family with all the attendant negative consequences.

The National Institutes of Health indicate that in 2008, 40 percent of babies were born to single mothers, up from 26 percent in 2002. That's a persuasive bit of evidence of a recently changing lifestyle. It is, however, not quite as dramatic as it appears. The increase may reflect a trend toward increased cohabitation instead of deadbeat dads or teen mothers. There appears to be a trend toward waiting to get married until after a child is born. The Census Bureau indicates that the percentage of households headed by a single parent showed little variation from 1994 through 2006. That percentage held at about 9 percent, up from 5 percent in 1970.

Capitalist abundance and freedom of choice have had a variety of impacts on *sloth*. They have enabled people to earn a satisfactory living with fewer hours of work than were required in earlier generations. Some people have used the resulting free time in a way that has made "couch potato" a synonym for sloth. But capitalism has also provided the time, opportunities, and incentives to gain riches, to express talents, and to achieve the status that so many people crave. The competition produced by those capitalist opportunities and incentives has often created a veritable frenzy of activity. Some observers in China have said that the Chinese now want to work all the time. Similar comments were made earlier about South Korea when it was shifting to capitalism. That competitive frenzy seems to exist today in the United States among many young people trying to get a head start in the race for the better schools and better jobs. Capitalist abundance and freedom allow us to choose sloth or achievement.

I have described three of the ways that capitalist abundance and freedom of choice have dramatically expanded the variety of lifestyles. But there is yet another dimension of change. Changing lifestyles alter the way people think about themselves and how they relate to other groups. New attitudes frequently bring conflict between people and groups. These changing ways of thinking may have been a factor in the race riots, the women's-lib movement, and the sexual revolution in the United States. Adjusting to changing lifestyles and ways of thinking can be difficult in an advanced country. To authorities in a rigid, religion-dominated country such as Iran or Saudi Arabia, the thought of facing the changes in lifestyle and attitude that they have seen in advanced capitalist countries is frightening. That is one reason they will continue to resist taking the steps necessary to gain the capitalist abundance many of their people desire.

The Three Capitalist "Sins"

The next three sins are intimately intertwined with capitalism: *greed*, a strong desire to gain material wealth; *pride*, the desire to be more important than others; and *envy*, a painful awareness of an advantage enjoyed by another, coupled with an intense desire to enjoy the same advantage. These three sins are manifestations of self-interest, an almost universal trait. Self-interest is the major driving force in a capitalist economy. It is highly effective. Of course, it can be carried to an undesirable extreme. Socialists viewed this aspect of capitalism as destructive. They wanted an economic system that encouraged, and relied on, community interest rather than self-interest.

Competitive capitalism can be harsh. When left entirely untempered by government, it can be brutal. *But capitalism gives people the courage and means to demand and get democracy, and democracy tempers capitalism.* In the future, the harshness of those three "sins" that are manifestations of self-interest will depend on the ability and willingness of the governments that we elect to temper competitive capitalism. Will people growing up in such a competitive environment elect a compassionate government? History indicates that they will. Under capitalist democracies people have generally elected governments that have softened the outcome of competitive markets with an array of social services. The selection of those services has not always been wise, and the quantity has sometimes been excessive, sometimes inadequate, but they have been sufficient to produce societies far more humane than socialist (government-managed) economies have been. Those three sins that are part of self-interest have not prevented the *virtues* of generosity and charity from shining through. Most important, self-interest under capitalism provides the productivity that makes possible the implementation of that generosity and charity. Socialism could not provide the resources to do so. In the end, socialism was much harsher than capitalism. A government cannot be truly *compassionate* unless it is teamed with an economy that is highly *productive*. Also, when governments keep labor and capital markets free from monopoly, self-interest generates competition that disciplines participants in the marketplace. Capitalist markets transmute competition into cooperation.

Transmuting Competition into Cooperation

Cooperation among people is the magic requirement for getting things done. Many forms of organization have been tried to gain that precious cooperation, but none have come close to achieving the cooperation that has come from the *competition* of capitalist markets. Socialists argued that improved productivity could be achieved by eliminating the competition of capitalism in favor of the cooperation of a socialist system. It was a disaster. People would not cooperate just because they were told to do so. In the Union of Soviet Socialist Republics, for example, business firms often had to keep several months' inventory of supplies on hand because they could not count on cooperation from their suppliers to deliver goods when promised. In capitalist economies, a few days' inventory is often sufficient because suppliers are driven by competition to deliver goods when promised. The enormity of the worldwide cooperation achieved by competitive capitalism is simply mind-boggling. And as this book has repeatedly described, capitalism is still an adolescent, having just recently emerged from a defective childhood on the way to a much improved maturity.

Warfare has often been used in the past to try to force widespread groups into a cooperative empire. Authoritative governments have been used by most countries to try to force cooperation. Religious persuasion has not been able to gain adequate cooperation except occasionally in very small groups. Competitive capitalism has gained remarkable cooperation among many people, but it needs help. As Chapters 4 and 5 described, governments are required to provide a favorable environment for competitive markets. Governments must guarantee adequate demand and intense competition. Also governments must compensate for capitalism's inevitable income inequality by helping to provide some social services, as described in Chapter 8.

If you have been counting and find one of the seven deadly sins missing, it's *wrath*, inappropriate feelings of hatred or anger. It is missing because I am not sure whether it is mostly encouraged or discouraged by capitalist abundance and freedom of choice.

Capitalism and Upward Mobility

The United States has long had a "rags to riches" tradition. Any young person, it has been believed, can achieve the American dream of reasonable success by hard work, courage, and determination. This tradition was fostered by the availability of "free" land up till late in the nineteenth century when the frontier closed. It has also been fostered by the opportunities available in American capitalism, the most capitalist of all large countries. Are the opportunities for upward mobility diminishing, and if so, how will America's democracy be affected?

The requirements for success have been changing. In largely agrarian America the qualities that led to success *for most people* were physical strength, stamina, endurance, dexterity, health, and attractive appearance, together with a kind of intelligence that can be called "common sense." Common sense is an ability to observe the world and the people in it and recognize the things that work and the things that fail. It is the ability to understand events that occur *in normal human activity*, as opposed, for example, to figuring out how electrons behave in a power grid. But in the twentieth century, technical knowledge proliferated. America industrialized, and things got a lot more complicated. Now success often requires a more complex kind of intelligence, including a memory that allows the storage of a huge amount of information, the ability to use that information to solve problems, the ability to analyze abstract concepts, the ability to articulate ideas, and other related capabilities. Talents for handling intricate social situations have also become more important as society has become more complex. The physical factors, except health, dexterity, and attractive appearance, are generally of less importance than they have been at any time in human history.

Under the changing requirements for success, a growing percentage of the population does not have the capability of earning a satisfactory living as evidenced by the rise in means-tested welfare. And a much larger percentage is finding *greater difficulty* in earning a satisfactory living. These people can vote. That can be a dangerous situation. Chapter 1 cited Alan Greenspan's worry that these conditions might lead to widespread resentment, political clashes, and misguided economic policies that work to the detriment of the economy and society as a whole. What should be done?

Of course, education and training are major parts of the solution. Judging from the fact that almost 41,000 *qualified* applicants for nursing schools were rejected in 2007 due to a *shortage of schools*, at a time when the shortage of nurses is damaging the quality of health care, the United States has not yet properly recognized the need for more comprehensive job-related schools and training.

Maintaining *very* full employment is, of course, another essential part of keeping alive the American tradition of upward mobility. We have made enormous progress in maintaining full employment. But, as Chapters 4 and 5 indicated, opportunities are still available to move up a notch to *very* full employment.

Yet another factor must be revisited. Ongoing globalization has thrown low-skill workers into competition with billions of such workers around the world. That competition shows up as sharply rising imports of high labor content goods and as a flood of unskilled immigrants (mostly illegal). As capitalism spreads around the world, upward mobility in today's emerging countries will dramatically increase with improved education and with the availability of better jobs. Competition to America's low-skill workers from those billions of low-skill workers (who will become skilled) will diminish. That promise will be realized but not quickly.

Put another way, competition between America's workers and workers throughout the rest of the world will be spread out more evenly between skilled and unskilled workers. Competition between unskilled workers will diminish and competition between skilled workers will increase. And that is another reason why the United States must put expanded emphasis on job-oriented education and training.

Globalization is providing the best opportunity this world has ever seen for peace and prosperity. It must be encouraged. Since low-skill workers currently pay the greatest price for globalization, every effort should be made to improve their employment prospects. The Earned Income Tax Credit, an improved No Child Left Behind school program, efforts to maintain *very* full employment, and many programs in our means-tested welfare system are useful ways to recognize our obligation to those who are bearing the greatest cost of globalization. Perhaps an expansion of our Trade Adjustment Assistance (TAA) program is warranted, although it is extremely difficult to administer. That program is designed to ease the transfer to new jobs of workers displaced by foreign competition. TAA provides extended unemployment benefits while retraining, temporary help in paying medical insurance, and, for those over 50, temporary subsidies to help offset lower pay in the new job. Of course, tough love should be an element in the programs to help the unskilled improve their skills. We should demand that recipients of aid do their part in improving their skills.

A Long-Term View:
The Accumulation of Human Knowledge

Learning is a major theme of this book about capitalism. We should therefore look to see how capitalism fits into the long-term accumulation of human knowledge. I divide accumulated knowledge into two parts—*technological and organizational*. The pool of technological knowledge is easily identified. It includes all those discoveries and inventions from before the wheel to after the transistor. The pool of organizational knowledge is more fascinating and challenging. It includes an understanding of all those aspects of human society that affect relations among people. Families, tribes, religions, customs, traditions, laws, courts, governments, and so on are the institutions that dominate the pool of organizational knowledge.

Developments Over Thousands of Years

Intelligent, curious, inventive human beings have been grinding out new products and better ways of producing them for millennia. The pool of *technological* knowledge has, over those thousands of years, grown inexorably, although for a long time, slowly. Lately, under capitalism, it has grown at astonishing speed. The pool of *organizational* knowledge, describing how people live and work together, has grown more slowly with more setbacks and with less assurance of success. For several millennia, authoritarian governments and religions were the dominant *large-scale* players active in the pool of organizational knowledge. But gradually a third player—the market—intruded into the organizational space.

It began with the appearance of specialists. Those people who could produce one product better than other people produced more than they needed. They traded part of their output for products produced by superior producers of other goods. As technologies increased the *variety* of goods, specialists proliferated and something happened—the market came into being. Pockets of traders arose along seacoasts, rivers, and land routes. Markets were not deliberately designed. They appeared naturally to fill the need for trade among specialists. They represented embryonic capitalism. As the variety of goods expanded thanks to that growing pool of technological knowledge, markets widened as a result of what I called in Chapter 3 the geographic law of specialization: the greater the variety of goods produced, the wider the trading area necessary to find the specialists to produce those goods. The efficiencies of markets improved. Banks arose to facilitate financing. Laws developed to facilitate necessary contractual relations.

The Last Few Centuries

In the pool of organizational knowledge, authoritarian governments began to feel a few pinpricks from democratic ideology. But those authoritarian governments gave up little power. Finally, however, a major new force entered that pool of organizational knowledge. Adam Smith and others recognized that the competitive market could be an extremely effective organizational device to channel the troublesome self-interest inherent in most people into a dynamic effort to serve a worldwide cooperative community. Capitalism entered the pool of organizational knowledge. It was not fully formed nor understood. But it survived because it worked, not beautifully, but far better than the alternative: government management of trade among specialists.

Over the last few centuries, the pool of organizational knowledge has been dominated by the interplay of authoritarian governments, religions, competitive markets (capitalism), and the upstart spirit of democratic yearnings. Chapter 1 of Fareed Zakaria's book *The*

Future of Freedom is an excellent guide to the intricate interactions of these protagonists of organizational knowledge over the past few centuries.[16] He quite properly emphasizes the need for economic freedom to *precede* democracy if that democracy is to survive and be effective.

The Period of Awakening

In just the last two decades of the twentieth century, competitive market principles (capitalism) began taking command of the pool of organizational knowledge. Those capitalist principles have become much more effective as countries have improved their management of aggregate demand and structural competition to provide a better environment in which markets can flourish. The primary economic antagonist—socialist ideology—is in full retreat due to its many failures recently unveiled.

Competition among governments to achieve capitalist abundance by attracting capital investment is gradually but inexorably forcing governments to adopt policies that will expand competitive markets. Civil liberties and genuine democracy will follow. Authoritarian governments will continue to put up a powerful rearguard action, but they will continue to see restrictions on their ability to govern.

That will leave religion as the sole survivor of the large-scale players that dominated the pool of organizational knowledge for millennia. What is capitalism doing to religion? Peace and tolerance are required to attract capital investment. This will gradually end the militancy of most institutionally sponsored religious zealots and will reduce the dictating of harsh behavioral codes by religion-dominated governments.

The worldwide trade and migration brought about by capitalism's need for wide markets will, over a long period, bring *competition* to religion as people find that under capitalist-required tolerance they can choose among various faiths with which they come into contact. That should improve the performance of various religions. It is not a coincidence that the United States has the most active religious community among historically Christian countries. Competition among religions in the United

States has existed almost from the beginning. That competition has forced religious establishments to better serve the needs of their members. It will take a long time, but competition among religions, intensified by worldwide trade and migration, should vastly improve the nature of the world's faiths.

As this is written, religion is coming under intense critical scrutiny. One can hardly watch the developments in the Middle East (and some other spots on earth) without developing a disgust for the hatreds and conflicts that religions have spawned. Many people are expecting and hoping for a decline in religious faith around the world as it has been declining in Europe. But religion has an important role to play. It will likely survive and prosper as it improves under capitalist competition and world integration.

In advanced capitalist economies with small families and constant movement between jobs and locations, people may become rootless. There will be few brothers, sisters, uncles, aunts, and cousins, and those few will often be scattered. Everyone needs a sense of belonging, preferably to a group with similar beliefs and aspirations. Religion can fill that need. Humans are meaning-seeking creatures. We search for meaning in everything around us. That includes life itself, and it invites the answers that religion offers. Religion can also fill the important function of giving hope and comfort to the inhabitants of this savage earth. And religion, improving under competitive pressure, will continue the critical function of teaching the rules by which people can live and work together in harmony.

In Conclusion

To repeat, every glint of optimism expressed throughout this book is based on faith in the learning process: an appraisal of what we have learned, the speed with which we are learning, and the competitive forces that are driving us to continue to learn. Both people and governments have learned and are continuing to learn at accelerating speed. Much of the pessimism so frequently expressed in the media appears to be based on the conviction that people and governments will not learn. Overoptimism is deadly. But valid optimism is necessary to keep the struggle alive. People huddled under a dark blanket of pessimism will not have the initiative necessary to solve our problems. Counsels of despair should be avoided. The wind is at our backs.

Can anyone read the history of the American twentieth century and *not* conclude that we have learned an immense amount that has improved the management of the market economy? And is there anything in that history indicating that that learning process is now at an end? Improvements will not come easily. But they will come as we get rid of more of those bad ideas that have hampered the world's development for centuries. Knowledge is power.

...And Beyond

Does the analysis in this book help us probe the mysteries lying beyond the capitalist century? Not much! That belongs to the science writers. With few constraints on the elastic limits of fertile imaginations, spectacular projections are appearing in print. They are especially noteworthy when dealing with the possibilities of technology modifying the capabilities of the human mind. In a hundred years or so, accelerating technological discoveries will undoubtedly create wondrous things. What they will be, we do not know. But an exciting adventure lies ahead.

END NOTES

[1] Alan Greenspan, *The Age of Turbulence: Adventures in a New World*, The Penguin Press HC, 2007.

[2] Marcus Walker, "Sweden Clamps Down on Sick and Disability Pay," *Wall Street Journal*, Vol. 249, No. 108, May 9, 2007, pp. A1-A15.

[3] Fareed Zakaria, *The Future of Freedom*, New York, W.W. Norton, 2003.

[4] Anatol Lieven and John Hulsman, *Ethical Realism: A Vision for America's Role in the World*, Pantheon, 2006.

[5] Anne-Marie Slaughter, "The Real New World Order," *Foreign Affairs*, Vol. 76, No. 5, September/October 1997, p. 184.

[6] Matthew D. Shapiro and Joel B. Slemrod, "Consumer Response to Tax Rebates," *American Economic Review*, Vol. 93, No. 1, 2003, pp. 381–396; Also, Shapiro and Slemrod, "Did the 2008 Tax Rebates Stimulate Spending?" Prepared for session on "Heterogeneity in the Response of Consumption to Income" American Economic Association Annual Meetings, San Francisco, CA, January 2009.

[7] Jonathan A. Parker, David S. Johnson, and Nicholas S. Souleles, "Household Expenditure and the Income Tax Rebates of 2001," *American Economic Review*, Vol. 96, No. 5, 2006, pp. 1589-1610.

[8] Jonathan A. Parker and Christian Broda, "The Impact of the 2008 Tax Rebates on Consumer Spending: Preliminary Evidence," mimeo University of Chicago, GSB, July 2008.

[9] Steven R. Shaw, "Slow Learners and Mental Health Problems: Over-Represented and Overlooked." In A. Canter, S. Carroll, L. Paige, & I. Romero (Eds.), *Helping children at home and at school: Handouts from your school psychologist* (Second Edition). Bethesda, MD: National Association of School Psychologists, 2004.

[10] Caroline M. Hoxby, "Achievement in Charter Schools and Regular Public Schools in the United States: Understanding the Differences," Harvard University and National Bureau of Economic Research, December 2004.

[11] Ezekiel J. Emanuel, *Healthcare, Guaranteed: A Simple, Secure Solution for America*, PublicAffairs, 2008.

[12] Rebecca M. Blank, "Evaluating Welfare Reform in the United States," *Journal of Economic Literature*, Vol. 40, No. 4, December 2002, pp. 1105-1166.

[13] "Cradle Snatching: The Difficulties of Living with a Low Birth-Rate," *The Economist*, March 16, 2006.

[14] Ben J. Wattenberg, *Fewer: How the New Demography of Depopulation Will Shape Our Future*, Chicago, Ivan R. Dee, Publisher, 2006.

[15] Robert P. Bremner, *Chairman of the Fed: William McChesney Martin Jr. and the Creation of the American Financial System*, Yale University Press, 2004.

[16] Fareed Zakaria, *The Future of Freedom*, New York, W.W. Norton, 2003.

INDEX